From Children's Interests to Children's Thinking

Using a Cycle of Inquiry to Plan Curriculum

Jane Tingle Broderick and Seong Bock Hong

National Association for the Education of Young Children
Washington, DC

National Association for the
Education of Young Children
1313 L Street NW, Suite 500
Washington, DC 20005-4101
202-232-8777 • 800-424-2460
NAEYC.org

NAEYC Books

**Senior Director, Publishing
and Professional Learning**
Susan Friedman

Director, Books
Dana Battaglia

Senior Editor
Holly Bohart

Editor
Rossella Procopio

Senior Creative Design Manager
Henrique J. Siblesz

Senior Creative Design Specialist
Charity Coleman

**Publishing Business
Operations Manager**
Francine Markowitz

Through its publications program,
the National Association
for the Education of Young
Children (NAEYC) provides a
forum for discussion of major
issues and ideas in the early
childhood field, with the hope
of provoking thought and
promoting professional growth.
The views expressed or implied
in this book are not necessarily
those of the Association.

Permissions

NAEYC accepts requests for limited use of our copyrighted material.
For permission to reprint, adapt, translate, or otherwise reuse and
repurpose content from this publication, review our guidelines at
NAEYC.org/resources/permissions.

Purchasers of *From Children's Interests to Children's Thinking: Using
a Cycle of Inquiry to Plan Curriculum* are permitted to photocopy the
checklists and blank cycle of inquiry forms on pages 134–147 in the
Appendices for educational or training purposes only. Photocopies
may be made only from an original book.

Photo Credits

© Getty Images: Cover

Courtesy of Jane Broderick: 9, 10, 11, 14, 21, and 81

Courtesy of Jane Broderick and Su Lorencen: 124

Courtesy of Seong Bock Hong: 63

Courtesy of Megan Felker: 31 (children's artwork)

Courtesy of Su Lorencen: 8, 23, 24, 26, 30, 32,
33, 34–35, 42, 50, 67, 92, 93, and 94

Courtesy of Deb Oglesby: 130

Courtesy of Christina Raffoul and Freda Shatara:
52, 53, 54, 55, 57, 58, 59, 69, and 127

Courtesy of Angela Venier: 83

**From Children's Interests to Children's Thinking: Using a Cycle of
Inquiry to Plan Curriculum.** Copyright © 2020
by the National Association for the Education of Young Children.
All rights reserved. Printed in the United States of America.

Library of Congress Control Number: 2019955317

ISBN: 978-1-938113-63-5

Item 1145

Contents

Preface

During our graduate studies, we were teaching assistants at the Reggio-inspired Early Childhood Laboratory School (ECLS) at the University of Massachusetts, Amherst. This was one of the first American settings to adapt and apply the early practices from the schools of Reggio Emilia, Italy. We learned to use documentation as a framework for developing curriculum and supported preservice teachers in this process. We were inspired to develop the cycle of inquiry (COI) forms discussed in this book after the first of three documentation conferences (2001–2003) held at the lab school. Each conference focused on interpreting children's thinking and the meaning of their play within one small video clip of play. Following an introductory session on the purpose of video documentation, participants met in breakout sessions to learn this process of interpreting children's play. As facilitators of breakout sessions, we realized that teachers came to this conference with an idea that Reggio-inspired curriculum centers on long-term projects related to children's interests. In these sessions, we experienced teachers digging deeply and gaining a lot of insight about children's thinking. Yet they were puzzled as to how to extend children's learning based on their interpretations of what the children were thinking and understanding. We knew they needed a guiding tool to develop curriculum from video observations or from observations in general. So we developed COI forms to bring to the 2002 conference. These were designed around the planning practices we experienced at the ECLS, where the teaching team of director, teaching assistant, and preservice teachers documented their thinking, their theories about the meaning of observations of children's play, their questions for guiding next steps, and their overall plan that emerged from their thinking about children's thinking. Attendees were delighted by the organization of the COI forms that guided their thinking process from observations to interpretations to questions that led to a provocation plan they could implement. Following the great successes with using the COI at these conferences, we realized these tools could be helpful to a broad community of educators seeking ways to implement inquiry with children that is inspired by the Reggio Emilia approach. Since 2003, we have been using the COI in our teacher education courses at East Tennessee State University and the University of Michigan–Dearborn and for professional development with early childhood programs in the field. We are often approached by teachers who are observing children carefully but still find it difficult to develop long-term projects. Amber Foster, a teacher and pedagogical coach we have worked with, says this about the impact of the COI on her work with children:

" This process of using the COI system has opened my mind into just how deep you can take one aspect of your project work. Previously, I would have just set out one initial provocation with our 4- to 5-year-old children and then moved on. When we began using the COI system, we were observing children carefully, yet wondering how to extend project work. We had been developing inquiry with children, posing questions with them around interests we'd observed, like their curiosity about the tree frog, our classroom pet. We formed a discussion with them sharing photos of the tree frog and asking what they'd noticed. They were intrigued by the way the tree frog hangs on the wire to go up to the heat lamp and wondered how and why this occurs. Their theory was that the frog has sticky hands, and they wanted to test out how to make their hands into sticky hands. A small core group of children thought of items like tape, glue, and Velcro dots to put on their hands and test their theories about what is best for sticky hands. Prior to using the COI system, we wouldn't have extended this learning past the first sticky hands experience. By using one series of COI forms, however, I was able to record and see so many more details and create curriculum action questions to explore several more aspects of their thinking, like the relationship between weight and stickiness and what their understanding of that was. Using this process has opened my eyes to see how this one documentation form, interpretation, and action questions can allow us to really extend and take children's understanding and thoughts to a whole new level.

In this book you will read about slowing down to record the unfolding details of play that represent children's competency and inquiry and about organizing curriculum around your observations to further their thinking. We want this work to inspire you so much that you want to share it to spark new conversations with children, colleagues, and families.

The Cycle of Inquiry Process

Children observe, experiment, explore, and form ideas about their world every moment of their day. Being witness to children's deep-felt curiosity and having the presence of mind to be in the moment and thinking with children is magical. It makes you want to jump in to photograph what is happening and record children's conversations to highlight their significance. When you make children's learning visible through documentation like this, do you notice the impact of these moments for you? How do they help you support children's continued interest in questioning, discovering, and learning? Looking carefully at what has captured your attention and sparked your curiosity is a first step in designing curriculum that emerges from children's inquiry.

Emergent curriculum is described as a continuous cycle of ongoing learning opportunities that emerge from teachers' careful observations of children's interests and thinking (Broderick & Hong 2011; Jones 2012). We adopted the term *emergent inquiry curriculum* to describe a curriculum that values teachers' thinking—their inquiry as to the meaning of children's play and explorations—and their development of next steps for learning based on their inquiry and questioning with children (Wien & Halls 2018). The cycle of inquiry (COI) system discussed in this book guides emergent inquiry curriculum. It embraces the ways children learn best. It is a tool for you to plan curriculum in response to children's curiosity and questioning, acknowledging the problems children encounter and identify as they act on their questions and taking seriously the solutions they hypothesize in relation to their experiences.

Children as Inquirers

The COI draws on children's natural sense of curiosity and questions about their world. Creating a path of learning that follows children's interests is often called *inquiry-based learning*. In a major study of research on how children learn best, the National Research Council (NRC 1999) found that they learn through the same processes that guide scientists in their research practices. These processes are currently the frameworks for the Next Generation Science Standards (NGSS 2019) and are highlighted here with examples of activities involving bluegrass music (a preschool inquiry studied in depth in this book), looking for worms, building with blocks, and balancing a mobile.

- Ask questions and define problems:
  - > When exploring the instruments used in bluegrass music, children *ask questions* about what makes their sounds so different from one another when all have strings that are used to make the sounds.
  - > Children *define the problem* of why the instruments sound different by developing hypotheses as to whether the size or shape of the instruments affects the differences in sounds.

- Develop and use models:
  - > Children create a *model* of music that peers can read and play by representing the sounds of a set of handbells with color-coded marks on a page that match the same seven colors of the bells.
  - > By drawing their ideas about where they think they'll find worms on the playground, children create a model that is a map representing their knowledge of the playground in relation to their current theories about locations of worms.

- Plan and carry out investigations:
  - With the map to guide their quest, the children *plan investigations* as they decide where to dig to locate worms on the playground.
  - They *carry out investigations* as they dig based on their map and plan.

- Analyze and interpret:
  - The children then *analyze* the findings of their search for worms, making notes on their map comparing where they found worms and where they thought they would find worms.
  - They also *interpret* the movement of these worms, using their findings to choose new methods for exploring the ways the worms will respond to their touch.

- Use mathematical and computational thinking:
  - As children build a tall tower or a bridge, they *use mathematical thinking* about shapes and how many blocks are needed.
  - They *use computational thinking* to determine the most efficient way to balance several items on either side of a mobile.

- Engage in argument from evidence:
  - Children *engage in argument from evidence* when they tell their friends why a precariously balanced set of blocks will fall over.
  - They also *engage in argument from evidence* to explain to friends that their hypotheses about finding worms in some locations did not match their findings.

These practices are inherent in curricula that value the opportunities for learning in everyday experiences. They also illustrate the importance that competent adults and peers have in facilitating children's learning (Bodrova & Leong 2006; NRC 1999; Pianta & Hamre 2009; Wood, Bruner, & Ross 1976). For example, as an effective teacher using the COI, you would recognize the learning opportunity embedded in children's desire to hunt for worms on the playground, providing paper and pencils for them to map out their theories as to where to locate these worms and then revisiting the maps with the children to discuss what they found (Lange, Brenneman, & Mano 2019). You would intentionally encourage the processes of modeling, collecting evidence, and analyzing as ways to direct and structure the children's inquiry toward more complex thinking and development (Bronfenbrenner & Ceci 1994; Fisher 2011; NRC 1999). Understanding that children's questions play a vital role in their learning, you would encourage them to continue to be curious and ask questions. As you use the COI, consider who is asking the questions in your classroom and how often you are empowering children to question and generate pathways for curriculum.

Teachers as Researchers

Careful observations are the first component of the COI process. You will design emergent inquiry curriculum in response to what you reflect on in your detailed observations of children. Observation records have been essential artifacts in early childhood education since the first child laboratories were developed in the early twentieth century, when the study of children was in its infancy. The observations in these early settings provided theoretical knowledge about the way children respond to their environment (Ginsberg & Opper 1988; Piaget [1926] 1997, [1947] 2003; Vygotsky [1934] 1986). Observations show whether children are capable of specific observable behaviors that are identified as standards, such as being able to take turns in conversation or coordinate movements in work that requires complex fine motor skills (Boehm & Weinberg 1996; Nilsen 2016). Teachers all make decisions about what they will do tomorrow in relation to what they have noticed about the way children behave today, designing adjustments based on their observations of children (Curtis 2017).

Teachers typically document children's behavior to assess developmental learning outcomes, each according to a standard, and use these observation records as a general guide for curricular planning. The thinking processes of children are not observable behaviors; therefore, they are typically not recorded by teachers. Yet children's thinking is directly linked to what they are learning and how.

For example, as Jillian repeatedly draws a cat, she is *thinking*, and learning, about the body parts and shapes of the body. Her teacher, observing Jillian's actions over time, thinks Jillian is also trying to organize the lines on the page to represent each body part with appropriate proportion and placement. The teacher notes this, and from this inference she designs a curricular extension with clay and several photo images of cats in various positions. Her *teacher thinking* is that the manipulation of clay will help Jillian focus on the relationship of body parts to the shape of the body.

Teachers' thinking has an enormous influence on the curricular decisions they make. Teachers often search for the child's point of view, measuring this against their own perspectives to interpret and make meaning within the context of their classrooms. They learn about children's interests and develop hunches about children's questioning and provide materials in response to what they notice. The COI process enables teachers to capture this sort of thinking about children's thinking as an essential part of their curricular planning processes. The COI process is, therefore, an action research approach to planning curriculum. The COI system presented in this book asks you to become a teacher researcher (Baker & Davila 2018; Stremmel 2007), gathering observation data and honing skills for analyzing and interpreting the data to frame questions and hypotheses about children's thinking so you can design curricular extensions that link to and support children's thinking and inquiry. Through these processes you will become curious about and study your own teaching and learning and experience the joy of being an inquirer with children (Baker & Davila 2018; Stremmel 2007).

The COI System

This book introduces a COI system as a structure you can use to design emergent inquiry curriculum. We've adapted the phases of the COI system from the work of other individuals in the field of early childhood

who have also been inspired by the Reggio Emilia approach (Gandini & Goldhaber 2001; Stremmel 2007). What is unique about our COI system is that each phase represents your thinking processes, and five forms allow you to clearly break down and articulate your thinking processes for designing emergent inquiry curriculum:

- As you observe children carefully, you record their words and actions on the COI Observation Record form.

- Your observations lead you to think about and then record the meaning within the play you observed on the COI Interpreting Thinking form.

- You consider questions you and the children have that can guide the children's inquiry a bit further, brainstorming and recording these as curricular ideas on the COI Curricular Action Plan form.

- This brainstorming leads you to design a COI Inquiry Provocation Plan, where you narrow down these many ideas into a provocation for next steps in learning.

- Following the implementation of the provocation, you revisit the session and evaluate it as a learning experience for both you and the children using the COI Reflective Evaluation form.

Ideally, you will learn to focus on each thinking process in a progression that is outlined by the chapters in this book. You will practice working with all the phases in order each time you develop a plan from an observation. As you follow the steps of a COI process (see the figure on page 4), you will learn how to adapt the use of the forms to a flow that makes sense in your own setting. For example, you may observe particular play experiences for many days before moving on through the COI phases, and you may develop more than one curricular plan from these observations. You may also learn ways to add to previously developed COI forms as a method for extending the curricular plans, a process you will see in the incinerator project example followed throughout the book.

The Cycle of Inquiry Process

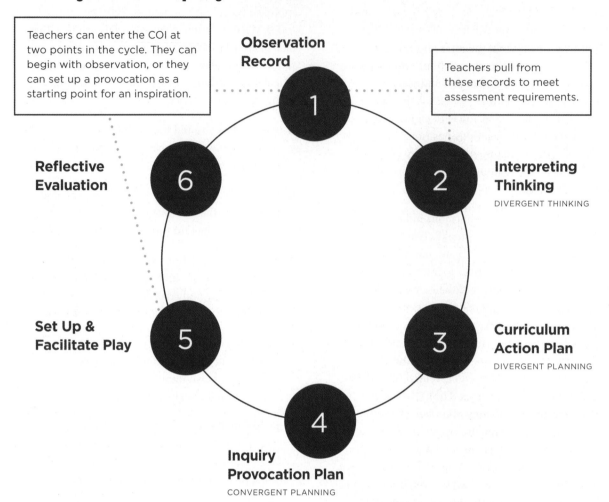

Teachers can enter the COI at two points in the cycle. They can begin with observation, or they can set up a provocation as a starting point for an inspiration.

Teachers pull from these records to meet assessment requirements.

Observation Record
1

Interpreting Thinking
2
DIVERGENT THINKING

Reflective Evaluation
6

Curriculum Action Plan
3
DIVERGENT PLANNING

Set Up & Facilitate Play
5

Inquiry Provocation Plan
4
CONVERGENT PLANNING

1. Observation Record: Teachers observe children's play and record observations (written notes, including photos, or using video) of children engaged in this play, asking questions about play that can lead to long-term inquiry.

2. Interpreting Thinking: Teachers reflect on observation data. They speculate on the children's minds—questioning what they know, what they are thinking, why they are doing things. Teachers consider play from the child's perspective.

3. Curriculum Action Plan: Teachers reflect on their observations and interpretations of play. They develop questions to learn more about the children and questions they imagine the children have in mind, and they add to questions the children pose. If teachers can write down what they are wondering about when they want to act on their thinking by intervening with a provocation, they have probably formed a good action question.

4. Inquiry Provocation Plan: Teachers develop plans to drive the curriculum forward—questioning which aspects of their curriculum action plans to organize for designing experiences where children's questions are just out of reach, their goals require a little something more to achieve, they are confounded somewhat, or their theories of the world are manifestly incomplete or unsatisfying. Children are drawn to explore in these settings when their interests are visible yet slightly challenged.

5. Set Up and Facilitate Play: Teachers facilitate in ways that allow children to do more and teachers to do less. They use observation records and photos or video to capture observations of the setup (provocation) and the children engaged in play.

6. Reflective Evaluation: Teachers reflect on their implementation of their intervention (provocation) to question children's engagement, identify evidence of learning and standards met, and consider what worked or needs improvement regarding their facilitation and documentation strategies.

Cycle of Inquiry Versus Project Approach: Key Differences

While both the COI process and the project approach seek to build on children's interests, there are differences between the two. The project approach is framed as a three-phase process of getting started, investigating, and concluding the project, often by holding a celebration. In the getting started phase, many teachers design anticipatory planning webs by gathering information about what children know and want to learn. These webs reflect topics teachers think will be meaningful to children based on their observations of the children's interests and conversations they have with the children.

For example, imagine children are interested in bluegrass music. The investigating phase of the project approach engages children in asking questions, in experiences with materials, and typically in experiences with experts in the field related to the study focus. Teachers introduce children to bluegrass music through singing, CDs, and video. They bring in musicians who perform for the children and engage them in the music. Through conversations, the teachers learn that the children want to perform as musicians and that children recognize the need for a stage for performing. Teachers invite the children to build the stage, and over a long period this process delves into construction thinking and terminology, leaving behind the bluegrass music focus. Then at the very end, with little time left before the preplanned celebration of the project, the children are asked to return to their bluegrass music focus, which by this time has become disconnected from their long-term construction process. The three-phase structure of the project approach has led the teachers to place the idea of a conclusion—performing bluegrass music for parents on a stage the children build—at the forefront of their minds at the start of the project. As in this situation, teachers using the project approach often plan for a project to conclude with a celebration around times in the calendar year for welcoming families into the classroom, which may limit the length of an investigation.

In a COI approach, teachers are uncertain as to the final direction of the curriculum. They continuously design next-step curricula from their observations and interpretations of children's thinking without a sense of where and when it might end or how it might unfold. In the bluegrass music study, for example, the teachers recognize that the major focus of the children's thinking is performing as musicians. Thus, teachers plan closely to this purpose by building a stage themselves as a teacher-initiated provocation to keep the children engaged in thinking of themselves as performers, realizing that asking the children to build a stage would guide thinking instead toward construction experiences.

In addition, teachers using a COI approach focus on children representing and re-representing their ideas with drawings, conversations, photographs, charts, dramatizations, and other media to construct knowledge of the concepts related to the topics they are researching. For example, children's conversations about stages and building them are the representations that feed teachers with the knowledge of what to include in their teacher-designed stage. This sort of representation and re-representation of concepts is less emphasized in project approach guidelines, although many teachers who implement the project approach encourage rich representations from children. Allowing the children in the bluegrass study to remain true to their performing focus leads to another type of representation—the children's writing of music, which becomes a strong thread of inquiry for the bluegrass study that you will read about in Chapter 3. Teachers with a high tolerance for ambiguity and a strong sense of adventure find the COI approach to be very exciting, creative, and satisfying.

How to Use this Book

Focus on one chapter at a time to learn about each phase of the COI, allowing yourself to gradually develop the reflective practice of making your thinking visible to you and others. At the end of each chapter you will find valuable prompts for revisiting the content in the chapter in relation to your current practice and recommendations for ways to share what you are learning with colleagues.

To help you get started, we begin the book by offering suggestions for setting up the classroom and establishing routines to support the COI. You'll revisit these setup processes repeatedly in later phases, after you reflect on what you observe and document. Here's what you can expect from each chapter:

- Chapter 1 guides you through the process of setting up your classroom learning environment at the start of the year, taking into consideration children's competency with materials, flexible spaces, open-ended materials, the aesthetic appeal of your classroom, small core group work, and the role of the classroom schedule in your planning processes.

- Chapter 2 provides a rationale for working with small core groups. You will learn to organize for whole group and small group classroom meetings to bring the thinking of small core learning groups to all within your classroom community and to help the children in small groups gain insights from the rest of their peers that will aid in their inquiry.

- Chapter 3 shares a preschool classroom's long-term explorations related to bluegrass music to give you an overview of the complex nature of emergent inquiry curriculum. Here you will learn about threads of inquiry, provocations, and Big Ideas as ways to cohesively organize the many ideas generated from children's explorations of a topic.

- Chapter 4 introduces you to observation practices that build on what you already notice and assess about children's developing skills. You will be invited to add to your practice by recording details that help you to think about the ways children's minds make connections and what they might be

thinking. This chapter guides you to slow down, make decisions about which experiences and interactions to observe, and consider the depth of detail for recording needed to better understand the meaning of these experiences for children. The COI Observation Record is introduced as a tool for you to record your initial thinking about your observations on children's thinking.

- Chapter 5 guides you to return to your observation records to think about the meaning of children's conversations and interactions. You may realize that you have been designing activities for children based on your thinking about their ideas and interests. The COI will guide you to *write down* these thoughts as interpretations of children's thinking. These data then account for your thinking as an influential component of your planning process and collaboration with colleagues in the reflective process.

- Chapter 6 asks you to brainstorm the many questions you have about what children know and question and to consider what you might want to further learn about the meaning in the play you've observed. You will be guided in this COI phase to consider several strategies you might use to encourage children to seek answers to their questions and solve problems they have encountered. This phase encourages you to think about many diverse approaches for following children's inquiry and the many possible materials you might consider for supporting them in their learning journey.

- Chapter 7 asks you to consider the diverse approaches you just designed in the previous phase of the COI process and to be mindful in choosing which of these ideas you will organize into a next-step plan—a provocation for the emergent inquiry curriculum with children. You'll then be guided to think about how to implement the provocation plan you just designed, discovering the many elements to consider when facilitating emergent inquiry curriculum.

- Chapter 8 explores reflective evaluation. This chapter provides a guide for reviewing and documenting your reflections on the experience you implemented with children based on your COI plan. You will consider how the children responded and what you learned that you can build on, and you will be excited to identify a wide range of learning standards the children are meeting.

- Chapter 9 shows how you can easily incorporate the documentation from each phase of your COI process into a documentation panel to communicate the story of the learning to children, colleagues, and families. This process will be illustrated by examples of documentation panels created by preschool teachers.

Emergent Inquiry Examples

Documenting your observation records and your planning thinking in each of the six phases of the cycle of inquiry transforms your thinking into action research data, linking your thinking and reasoning to children's thinking in your planning process.

Examples from a variety of real classroom settings are provided throughout the book to help you better understand the content by making the emergent inquiry curriculum come to life and to illustrate the COI process and the use of the forms. Three projects are examined in depth: a castle tower project, a bluegrass study, and an incinerator project.

A castle tower project is introduced in Chapter 2 to illustrate a classroom meeting around an element of the children's inquiry. In this mixed-age classroom of 3- to 4-year-old children, there was a lot of interest in castles. The upper and lower loft had been transformed into rooms of a castle, with the bottom portion being the kitchen and eating area. Many children were exploring various aspects of castle life, including the use of pulleys to pull items from the lower to the upper loft. In the block area, children used levers like those used to open castle gates, and a long-term focus centered on the construction of castle towers. The classroom meeting described in this chapter was used as a provocation initiated by the teachers for children to experiment with a variety of materials for building tall castle towers.

The bluegrass study introduced in Chapter 3 is a teacher-initiated emergent inquiry project that extended through an entire school year in a classroom of 4- to 5-year-olds in the Child Study Center, a laboratory school at East Tennessee State University. The teachers in this classroom were interested in developing their use of the COI to design curriculum framed around bluegrass music, a strong part of the local culture of the area. Many details of this study are shared as an example of the way an overarching Big Idea can extend into several threads of inquiry within a long-term emergent inquiry project. A documentation panel from the bluegrass study is highlighted in Chapter 9.

You will follow the progress of the third inquiry, the incinerator project, throughout the chapters that focus on the phases of the COI (Chapters 4–8). The development of this project by preservice teachers illustrates each phase of the COI. Like many of you reading this book, these teachers were engaging in their first experience with emergent inquiry curriculum. The project took place among 3- to 4-year-old children at the University of Michigan–Dearborn's Early Childhood Education Center. Large-format documentation panels from this project are also highlighted in Chapter 9.

Who this Book Is For

This book is designed to support a wide variety of early childhood educators in learning to implement emergent inquiry curriculum using a COI approach. Preschool teachers can follow the processes in the book to build on their existing skills. Administrators can use the book as professional development support for teachers. Teacher educators can use this as a textbook to guide preservice teachers in learning to develop curriculum for young children. The book is intended to nurture inquiry among all learners in the field of early childhood.

Whether you are a preschool teacher, a preservice teacher, or a teacher educator, you will want to understand the way the school year starts in an emergent inquiry classroom. As you read through the next chapter, you will learn some guidelines for setting up an early learning environment, creating a daily schedule to support emergent inquiry, and identifying a focus for an inquiry project.

CHAPTER 1
Setting Up the Classroom for Emergent Inquiry

Emergent inquiry is within your reach. Some basic principles for classroom design, scheduling, and planning for a long-term inquiry are outlined in this chapter. By the time you finish it, you'll have a clear understanding of how you can prepare your environment for this dynamic learning and teaching cycle. To get there, we'll begin by looking at the broad concepts involved in creating this space for inquiry in order to set a foundation. As you move through the cycle, you'll come back to the processes in this chapter again and again, acting on what you've learned by observing, documenting, and interpreting to extend the children's inquiry.

Learning Centers

An overall goal of arranging the environment for emergent inquiry curriculum is to organize learning spaces where children can be protagonists, independently developing relationships with people and using materials to translate their thinking and responses into many different languages, or ways of understanding and expressing their thinking about the world (Curtis 2017). Start by planning for learning centers organized around content that is typically identified as developmentally appropriate—that is, it promotes children's learning through practices that build on children's strengths and are appropriate to each child's culture, language, and abilities (NAEYC 2009). These centers might include a dramatic play center, a library center, a manipulatives center, a sensory center perhaps with a focus on science, a block center, a quiet center, and an art center. Then incorporate ideas from the following sections about designing flexibility within the spaces, providing open-ended materials, respecting and building on children's competence, and applying aesthetics to your design (Curtis 2017). Design centers for the start of the year that are relevant to

your context and to the children's lives. The examples in this section include a home living center, a writing center, an art center, and a manipulatives area.

Flexible Spaces

When you design each center flexibly, you can redesign them in response to children's interests and inquiry by adding or removing materials or furniture to accommodate the new concepts children are exploring. For example, teachers in the ongoing inquiry into bluegrass music initially set up their dramatic play center with home living materials: dining table, sink, stove, refrigerator, baskets of foods and dishes, and cloths and napkins. This center was located at the other end of the classroom from the block area. As the bluegrass inquiry progressed, the teachers' observations and reflections led them to redesign the dramatic play center. They created a stage (see below) in response to the children becoming familiar with bluegrass instruments and sharing their knowledge that people who play these instruments perform in bands on stages.

Bluegrass stage

From Children's Interests to Children's Thinking

In addition, the teachers moved the dramatic play center near the block area to open the center for more flexible play involving the block area. This allowed children to extend their thinking about using a bluegrass stage for performing to thinking about performing in a community or in various cities alongside the many roads children were continuously building. A variety of photos of bluegrass performers and instruments were also provided to spur children's thinking in the block area.

The top photo below illustrates the way teachers in one classroom creatively use a shelf to divide and link materials to two centers (writing and art) so that children can choose from a variety of marking tools for writing or creating artwork. The materials cart that is set in front of the metal easel, shown in the bottom photo below, divides the easel into two sections. This provides a visual cue that two children might work here—one on either side of the cart.

Shelf dividing art and writing centers

Easel in art center next to writing center

Dramatic play centers can be redesigned over and over to accommodate children's changing interests. Home living is often a first choice for a learning center early in the year as it draws on what may be familiar to children at home, allowing them to explore within the context of their family home and culture. The realistic and natural look of the kitchen home living center in the top photo below helps the children in this classroom context connect their representations to their experiences at home. Adapt the home living space to include items that represent the diverse family cultures in your classroom and the children's communities.

Home living center set up as a kitchen

In the block center shown in the photo below, the blocks are clearly organized according to shape. Having two building surfaces, the floor and a platform, allows a variety of ways for children to be comfortable and invites different types of thinking. The teachers in this classroom have added a variety of interesting materials on a shelf to the right of the platform, such as stones, cylinders, and wooden knobs, to encourage diverse approaches for children's constructions (see the photo on the following page).

Block center

Additional block center materials

These examples illustrate a few options where teachers intentionally considered the materials to present and ways to organize those materials in the centers to be inviting and to provoke creativity and inquiry (Curtis 2017). This is known as a *provocation*—the intentional setup of materials within a learning center to elicit the threads of inquiry, the learning that emerges from the children. Setting up provocations allows the children to do more on their own and encourages them to think of different ways of using the materials. When children have a variety of materials to investigate and can initiate their own activities, teachers have greater opportunity for using the COI practices of observation and documentation to support their reflection on the children's emergent learning. You'll learn more about provocations and threads of inquiry in Chapter 3.

Open-Ended Materials

While emergent inquiry teachers start off the school year with learning centers that are typical of many early childhood programs, their choices of materials are less commercial. Open-ended materials have the ability to transform from one purpose to another. A block can become a telephone, a vehicle, or a house. While open-ended materials challenge children to explore in diverse ways and to represent their thinking independently or in collaboration with peers, the ways a teacher intentionally sets up the materials can influence the types of thinking that might be explored.

Natural materials are favored open-ended choices in emergent inquiry settings. Think of incorporating branches into the block area where they might become trees or borders for roads, among many other possibilities. Branches in the art area might replace pencils to create an image with lines by dipping the end of the branch into paint. Pinecones or shells in a block area may lead to their use as people or to decorate complex block structures, and when they are placed in a bowl or pan in a home living center they can represent food. Arranging all these materials together in a quiet section of the room or in a manipulatives area will encourage children to touch them, experience and discriminate their textures, or sort according to patterns they notice. In these examples, teachers are helping children to understand that they can use familiar materials in new ways.

Children's Competence

Working with children around their inquiry leads you to recognize and value how much they know, their eagerness to investigate and explore, and their competence with materials. Emergent inquiry teachers recognize that children are competent with many materials that might not be found in typical early childhood classrooms, such as small paintbrushes; permanent artist-grade felt-tipped markers; high-quality art papers; and a large variety of paint colors. Introduce new materials to children by modeling in ways that allow children to learn the appropriate attitude for responsible use while also being able to explore the tool creatively with autonomy (Baker & Davila 2018). As you learn to observe with intention, you will gain insights into ways to model in relation to children's inquiry focus, which you will learn about in Chapters 4–7.

In small or whole group meetings, or with individual children, introduce materials like black pens, paint, or clay before you set them out for independent exploration. Use the tool or material yourself along with a think-aloud strategy of telling children what you are doing as you model the processes. For example, with an artist-grade fine-tip black pen, you might say, "As I draw without pressing hard on the pen, I get a thin line, and when I press harder the line gets darker and thicker. I don't want to press too hard, because I will bend or break the tip and I won't

From Children's Interests to Children's Thinking

be able to use the pen anymore. Here I am going to show you that when I try to draw with this pen where the tip has been broken, I can't make a mark."

It is important to introduce appropriate use of any tools prior to setting up a provocation in a learning center and to continue to guide children by asking questions that encourage them to think about why and how they are using a tool (Baker & Davila 2018; Lange, Brenneman, & Mano 2019; Shaeffer 2016). Your goal is to respect children's competence in their use of these tools as they represent their ideas in the context of the inquiry they are invested in.

Aesthetics

Reggio Emilia educator Vea Vecchi notes that aesthetics activates learning (2010). Children are inspired by beauty and order. Maria Montessori also understood that order and organization influence young children's interest and engagement (Crain 2011). Practice working with the concept of aesthetics in your classroom by focusing on your use of visual cues and the organization of materials in the learning centers.

Visual cues within a learning center guide children's thinking about how to enter and engage with autonomy, which allows teachers more opportunity to facilitate children's authentic experiences with the materials. Imagine setting up an invitation for children to paint a still life. You set a bouquet of flowers in the center of the table. At each of four seats you place a sheet of watercolor paper, a paintbrush, a folded washcloth for drying the paintbrush, a palette with small dabs of dried watercolor paint, and a small container of water. The materials will guide children to consider painting at that table and to potentially paint an image inspired by the flowers. The four pieces of paper visually suggest to children that four can work at this table. This setup is designed to encourage children to enter and engage without the need for your intervention.

The lack of clutter in an area establishes an aesthetic in which order is valued. Intentionally choosing to set out fewer materials helps children clearly see the materials, understand the purpose of the center, be more thoughtful in their choice of materials, and engage in collaborations with peers. For example, one of the shelves in a classroom's manipulatives center

is set up with one or two items per section in each shelf, with related items together, like the games on the bottom right in the photo below. Lattice room dividers separate this area from another learning space, and it is clear to the children that they can use these materials on the area rug in front of the shelf, only a small portion of which is visible in this image. Guiding children to maintain the order of the center helps them develop self-regulation skills related to meaningful use of the center.

Manipulatives center

The Daily Schedule

Another important feature for organizing your classroom at the start of the year is a daily schedule. Allow for long, focused investigation periods and clear routines that children can count on for communicating with peers in whole group experiences, some in which all will gather to discuss topics and processes related to the emergent inquiry. Teachers rely on the structure of the daily schedule to help children develop self-regulation in relation to their social experiences of the daily routines (Bronfenbrenner & Ceci 1994; Copple & Bredekamp 2009). The social routine of the schedule marks regular points in the day by which children can organize their understanding of time. Classroom meetings (discussed in Chapter 2) are significant segments of this routine schedule. The sample program schedules on this page illustrate the variety of approaches among emergent inquiry classrooms. Routine events in the daily schedule provide opportunities to focus on elements of the classroom setup. For example, since you and your coteacher are continually introducing new materials and redesigning learning centers to facilitate threads of inquiry, you can ask the children each morning what they notice that is new or different in the classroom.

Emergent inquiry teachers leave their provocations out for children to explore over extended periods of days and weeks, so the inquiry allows time for deep exploration. Teachers don't move all children through all activities. Small core groups focus on different aspects of an ongoing inquiry project, and on a daily basis many children play in centers not dedicated to the inquiry focus. Thus, all learning centers are designed with materials that will engage children deeply.

Sample Half-Day Program Schedule	
9:00 a.m.	Arrival
9:15	Informal classroom meeting with whole class ■ Welcome, attendance, weather, calendar ■ What do you notice in the room today?
9:30	Constructive playtime
11:00	Family-style snack (allows for conversation among peers and teachers)

11:15	Classroom meeting
	
	■ Informal classroom meeting two days per week:
	
	  • Social ritual experiences (who is in the classroom, singing, story, movement)
	
	■ Focused classroom meeting three days per week:
	
	  • Focusing on content from long-term project work

11:45	Outdoor play
12:30 p.m.	Pickup

Note: Focused classroom meetings can also be organized during constructive playtime with small core groups

Sample Full-Day Program Schedule	
7:30–9:00 a.m.	Arrival, constructive playtime for programs with very early drop-off (children choose where to play, and parents often stay to engage with children)

9:00	Classroom meeting
	
	■ **Informal classroom meeting** every day at the start of school and two to three days per week as focused classroom meetings develop:
	
	  1. Social ritual experiences (who is in the classroom, singing, story, movement)
	
	  2. What do you notice in the classroom?
	
	  3. Planning constructive play choices at the close of the meeting
	
	■ **Focused classroom meeting** two to three days per week as inquiry project unfolds (the meeting time can lengthen as children become engaged in project-related discussions and remain focused for longer periods of time):
	
	  1. Discussion focusing on content from long-term project work
	
	  2. Planning constructive play choices at close of meeting

9:30–10:20	Constructive playtime (children choose where to play; teachers facilitate small core groups with inquiry investigations)
10:20–10:30	Cleanup
10:30–11:30	Outdoor play
11:00–11:30	Morning session pickup
11:30–11:45	Transition indoors and prepare for lunch
11:45 a.m.–12:30 p.m.	Lunch and preparations for nap time
12:30	Nap time
1:30	Constructive playtime as individual children wake up
3:00	Classroom meeting focusing on closure for the day
3:30–5:00	Pickup (children are engaged outdoors or indoors, with only a few centers open in relation to number of children and adults present)

From Children's Interests to Children's Thinking

Identifying an Inquiry Focus and a Core Group of Interested Participants

After setting the stage for the emergent inquiry process with the learning environment and daily schedule, turn your attention to observing and documenting the ways the children interact in each of the carefully designed learning centers. You'll notice some of the children becoming deeply engaged in specific explorations. This will help you determine a possible inquiry focus. Coordinate observation time with your coteacher so that one of you can document in this focus area using running records, a camera or video camera, and the COI Observation Record (discussed in Chapter 4) while the other facilitates the flow of activity throughout the remaining centers.

The children who are the core players in the centers where early inquiries seem to be forming become the central investigators in the context of the inquiry (Weatherly, Olesan, & Kistner 2017). They will be the children you invite into the inquiry provocations you set up. This small core group might consist of about four to seven children who genuinely show interest in participating in the ongoing learning for the duration of a long-term project. On a day-to-day basis you might invite all or some of the small core group to engage in the inquiry work. At times you might choose to invite other children who may have ideas for enhancing or extending the project. You can determine the new children you will bring into the inquiry by observing their interest and recognizing specific skills and knowledge they have that could support the inquiry focus.

Take time to review your observations notes with your coteacher to reflect on the ideas you each have about the concepts that are capturing the children's attention. These become the seeds for generating an inquiry focus that you can guide and extend into many possible threads of inquiry by reorganizing the learning centers.

Redesigning Learning Centers Around a New Inquiry Focus for Long-Term Investigation

As you redesign your classroom to incorporate the emerging inquiry focus of the small core group, introduce materials slowly and carefully. Generally, there are no more than a few centers dedicated to the inquiry work. Other centers retain the day-to-day focus of typical developmentally appropriate preschool learning centers, offering materials and experiences that invite and challenge the children to explore, imagine, create, interact, and problem solve. In addition, your careful ongoing observation and documentation of children can lead to new threads of inquiry. Thus, a classroom can have more than one inquiry focus or centers where related threads of inquiry are explored by different small core groups (Weatherly, Olesan, & Kistner 2017).

In the following vignette, a classroom of 3-year-old children offers a good example of an intentional redesign of an art center where a portion of the center focuses on the inquiry and another part of the center remains open for other types of art explorations.

> Initially the art center is set up with a long wall of easel space where several children can paint and two adjacent tables for working freely with any of the materials within the art center. The children's interest in painting leads the teachers to design two provocations in the art area: a color-mixing provocation on one portion of the long easel space and a mark-making provocation on one of the tables in the center. These two threads of inquiry, painting and mark making, are explored using a variety of painting and drawing tools.
>
> The early phases of the painting inquiry involve guiding children through complex color-mixing processes, mixing and naming colors. Children develop ways to record the amounts of each color they use to mix a color so they can mix the same color again in the future.
>
> Next to the easel wall, the teachers make a space for directing children's attention to the diverse range of marks that can be created with markers and pencils. They invite children to post examples of their marks (top left photo on the following page) onto the wall beneath photo documentation of children engaged in

mark-making activities (not pictured). Children categorize similar marks into columns, and as they identify a name for each type of mark, teachers label the marks with pink sticky notes. Children refer to this as their "mark dictionary," which builds on the concept of Reggio Emilia educators (Edwards, Gandini, & Forman 2012) that children express themselves in many languages, one of which is marks.

To the right of the mark dictionary, teachers set up white sheets of quality watercolor paper to invite children to paint (see the bottom photo below). Patches of the child-invented colors are posted above this easel to inspire children to reference these colors, which are available in small jars near the easel (not pictured). Teachers intentionally place the mark dictionary to the left of this easel to encourage thinking about paint application as a form of mark making. A well-organized learning center that incorporates documentation of past and current explorations (see Chapter 9) communicates the learning processes to children, families, and visitors.

Even though two sections of the art center are designed around the inquiry project, these teachers leave a large work table available for children who have other forms of art in mind. The many materials that are always present for children's open-ended art experiences are organized clearly on the shelves, ready for them to initiate independently (see the top photo below).

Art center

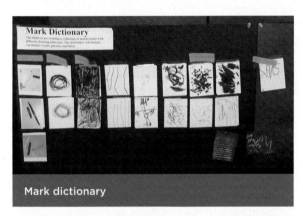

Mark dictionary

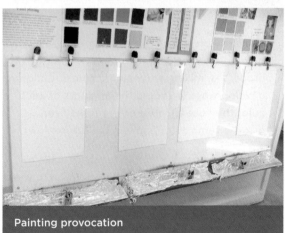

Painting provocation

Still-life drawing and painting provocation

From Children's Interests to Children's Thinking

In addition, these teachers reframe another center to accommodate the mark-making and painting inquiries, for a total of three areas devoted to this study. The children can visually read the intentions of the provocation, shown in the bottom right photo on the previous page. Two people can enter this special space and use a clipboard and pencil to draw the objects beautifully arranged in front of a mirror. The mirror might encourage children to look closely at the objects to notice the details from many perspectives. On the wall beside the still life are photographs of children carefully drawing the gourds; each photograph is aligned above the child's observational drawing and painting. Children can be inspired by the work of their peers when documentation is presented as part of a provocation.

For Further Reflection and Inquiry

With an understanding of how to begin setting up your classroom for emergent inquiry, you likely have ideas about possible learning flowing through the different learning centers. In the next chapter you'll discover how to use small groups and classroom meetings to spread the news about each center so that all children in the classroom have opportunities to learn from the long-term inquiry.

For deeper reflection on setting up the classroom environment for emergent inquiry learning, try these suggstions:

1. Look around your classroom and notice areas where you can remove clutter to make the space more inviting for children.

2. As you declutter, consider how each learning center is providing visual cues to children about how to use the center. How can you organize some materials in some centers each day as special invitations for children to play (think of the still-life provocation with flowers)?

3. If you sometimes find yourself preparing materials while children are waiting, brainstorm how you can have all materials ready for the children to use when it's time.

4. Focus on your classroom schedule and consider ways to redesign it to allow plenty of time for focused constructive play.

CHAPTER 2

Facilitating Classroom Meetings and Routines

Classroom meetings provide opportunities for teachers to bring children together. Many early childhood teachers refer to these whole group meetings as *circle time* or *whole group time*. It is beneficial to bring the group together in informal meetings to frame the start of the day, for transitions, and to close out the day. In addition to these introductory, transition, and closing meetings, teachers in emergent inquiry classrooms organize more focused meetings with a small core group of children or the whole group. These meetings center on aspects of a long-term project and sometimes serve to bring the ideas of the core inquiry group to the entire class.

Informal Classroom Meetings

Informal classroom meetings refer to those in which teachers gather children to focus on social topics like classroom rules, communication, and the solving of social conflicts and other problems and to experience social rituals such as singing and movement, reading books, and finger plays. Informal classroom meetings are typically brief and meant to support the organization of the day.

Early morning meetings, where teachers welcome children while also engaging them in the process of greeting their peers, are a prominent feature in most early childhood classrooms. Children develop an awareness of others and a sense of themselves as part of a community as they get to know their peers within the context of these social interactions. In many classrooms, teachers take time to ask children to take responsibility for roles or job assignments, such as snack helper, caretaker of plants, or caretaker of classroom pets, which helps children develop a social sense of community and responsibility.

In the informal classroom meetings in emergent inquiry classrooms, many preschool teachers ask children to share the things they noticed that are new in the classroom that day. As described in Chapter 1, you will introduce new materials and redesign learning centers regularly in response to the children's inquiry and to create provocations. Therefore, these changes can be a regular part of the conversation. Asking children to share about these changes opens up discussion about the new materials in certain centers and their purpose in relation to the kinds of play and explorations that have recently been occurring in those centers.

These discussions provide opportunity for teachers to review the ideas being expressed within each center during a long period of *constructive playtime*, a term many emergent inquiry teachers use instead of *free choice* or *free play*. The term *constructive* represents the idea that children are focused, learning, and constructing new understanding within the context of their play. For example, imagine that teachers discussed the use of clay coils for building castle towers in a whole group meeting on the previous day and that on this day, clay has been set anew in the art area for this purpose. When discussing what the children notice on this day, the teachers are able to reference the classroom meeting from the day before and reflect on photo documentation to revisit and guide the direction for engaging with clay in the art area. This is a conversation that both reflects on the past and also inspires ideas for the future.

Focused Classroom Meetings to Enhance Inquiry

While classroom meetings offer opportunities for cognitive richness and extending children's thinking, these opportunities are often missed even in high-quality early childhood classrooms (Hamre et al. 2014). Teachers may not have the time or, like Amber and her colleagues with the tree frog exploration example in the Introduction, may not be clear on how to extend interesting inquiry and focus their discussions beyond one simple experience. What is different in emergent inquiry classrooms is that the focus of whole group discussions goes beyond the notion that problem solving is limited to rules, social interactions, and conflict resolution. Emergent inquiry teachers plan for a few focused classroom meetings each week—sometimes with the whole group and sometimes with just a few children— centered on problems and questions aligned with threads of inquiry embedded in the children's constructive play experiences. Through careful planning, teachers can intentionally help children to meta-reflect—that is, reflect on their own thinking about their interests, their questions and curiosities, and the ways they see the world—by engaging in experiences and dialogue with peers. One classroom meeting began with the following dialogue and led to comparing the ways real castle towers were similar and different to Everett's tower:

> **Teacher:** (*Shows children photos of the castles they built in the block center on the previous day.*) Please tell us about the structure in this photo.
>
> **Everett:** It's a castle. There's the walls and the towers. The towers are not tall enough.
>
> **Teacher:** How can we help Everett think about making his tower taller?
>
> **Sydney:** Add more blocks on top.
>
> **Everett:** When I do, they fall.
>
> **Kathy:** But, those towers of yours are taller than the walls.

> **Teacher:** Let's look at these pictures of real castles with towers. What do you notice?
>
> **Everett:** That one is round. It's made of blocks like my tower.

When you organize focused classroom meetings, you are providing opportunities for the small core inquiry group to introduce their experiences and ideas to the whole group, sharing to solidify their understanding of the content and processes and to get new ideas from peers. This also allows you to guide the core group in posing problems they are facing to their peers to ask for help in finding solutions. Sharing their processes with the whole class exposes new children to the cognitively rich experiences that are occurring across the classroom, which may inspire new players to enter into the inquiry periodically or long-term.

Benefits of Focused Classroom Meetings

Gathering children together to focus on content from the small core group's inquiry processes is beneficial for

- Introducing the content to other children who might eventually participate in the project over time

- Providing the content to the entire class so the teacher can assess the interest and knowledge of the whole group regarding the topic and concepts

- Bringing new ideas from peers to children in the small core group

---

As you embark on your emergent inquiry journey, you will frequently organize focused classroom meetings to gather the joint attention of only the small core group on specific aspects of their inquiry. Sometimes these small group sessions can engage the group in dialogue that provides you with more insight into the thinking behind their constructive play. Other times you might have some materials, questions, or statements to share to nudge the children's thinking in new directions.

Through this back and forth, sharing information and ideas from small group to whole group, teachers can ensure that all children have been introduced to the content that is the focus of the inquiry. As an example, in one classroom the meetings were organized around a long-term story project that occurred over a period of about four or five months. The story project emerged from a whole group meeting where the teacher read a story about a boy and his father who left their city apartment to go on a hike into the woods. While reflecting on the story in the book, some children noticed a path in the woods and some mentioned that the story was a path. Several aspects of the inquiry project emerged in various centers during this time frame, like the process of drawing a line and using stamps to represent elements of the story, including the house, the trailhead, a bear or other animal on the path, and the lake at the end.

Still, there was a group of children who never entered any of these centers. These children primarily engaged in rich dramatic play experiences each day. To learn more about their play and consider ways to support their thinking, their teacher asked them if they would tell her the story of their play. Their response revealed that they had been paying close attention to the developments of the story project, because they immediately went to the art area to find materials they needed to draw renditions of their stories using symbols alongside curving lines, a method developed by other children in the story project process that had been shared during several focused classroom meetings.

The experience with this small group was very insightful. It validated the notion that all children will benefit and learn from an emergent inquiry curriculum that centers on a small core group. The focused classroom meetings offered two or three times each week in relation to story construction, dramatic performance of plays, and related content provided the teacher ample time to assess the learning of all children in relation to the inquiry content, even those who did not directly participate in the day-to-day project focus. As the year unfolded, the children engaged in classroom meeting discussions and processes for longer and longer periods of time, sometimes wanting to go beyond 45 minutes. In such cases, the teacher planned to continue the discussion on another day.

Guidelines for Planning a Focused Classroom Meeting

The guidelines that follow outline a process for you to intentionally plan a focused classroom meeting that emerges from your careful observations, your interpretation of the thinking and purposes within children's constructive play, and questions that emerge in response (a summary of the guidelines appears on page 20). This focused classroom meeting is a teacher-initiated provocation—one that is based on a teacher-generated interest that the teacher believes will deeply engage children's curiosity and support a long period of inquiry (see Chapter 3). The guidelines are followed by a classroom example showing how they can be put into action. All the steps around observation, documentation, and reflection are discussed in depth in the following chapters. As you read through them, you will learn to use the COI forms to guide you through the processes of designing emergent inquiry curriculum from your observations of children. As you learn to use the COI forms for documenting your observations and interpretations of play and the questions that emerge, you will be able to rely on them to design a plan for a focused classroom meeting.

1. Observe and Document

Observe children carefully, documenting their interactions with peers and materials using a written format with photos, or using video, which we will refer to as data. Review this documentation data to interpret and develop an understanding of the thinking and purposes behind the observed play. Think about the reasoning behind the children's play, the why and how of their actions and conversations (Wien & Halls 2018). What do you think they are thinking? What do you think they know, have misconceptions about, or question?

2. Identify a Question or a Problem to Pursue

Dig as deeply as you can to identify any questions the children might have or questions you might pose for them to guide their inquiry further. Can you identify a problem—one that is developmentally appropriate and of interest to many children—that could be pursued with the support of a group? The use of a focused classroom meeting to introduce a problem can be a teacher-initiated provocation intended to add new information to children's existing knowledge. The problem might also be in the form of a responsive provocation, where materials are provided in relation to the needs of children's ongoing inquiry to deepen their understanding of ideas they are already exploring.

3. Choose Materials that Will Intrigue and Allow Exploration of Problems and Questions

When planning for the focused classroom meeting, have materials prepared to frame the problem, pose the question, and explore the problem or question. Familiar materials can be explored in new ways, and new materials can be introduced (Baker & Davila 2018). These might include materials you have observed the children using or new materials to help the children find solutions to their questions or probe further. Follow their inquiry in such a way that children feel they are the authority in the process, making a seamless connection to their previous play (Baker & Davila 2018). Finally, plan for the ways you will document the group's thinking and learning.

4. Design a Setup that Will Capture Dialogue and Invite Exploration

Consider the best setting in the classroom to gather children for the focused classroom meeting. It might be your designated area for whole group discussions or the learning center that the discussion is focusing on.

Think about how the children will be seated, where to place the provocation materials so you can access them as needed, and what materials you will need for documenting the experience.

5. Form Questions that Will Probe and Extend Children's Thinking

Your intention as a facilitator during focused classroom meetings is to promote open dialogue with the children about their thinking. Use questions as prompts to generate these conversations, and encourage children to take the lead.

6. Design Procedures

Thinking through all you will need to successfully engage children in productive conversations around the inquiry project better prepares you to engage in a turn-taking conversational process with children. Your goal is to be ready to turn over the discussion to them, allowing them to take the lead in sharing findings from their learning center, solving problems, and posing new questions. You will serve as a facilitator to assist with the complexities of turn taking, listening, revisiting ideas, and introducing new materials and content that have potential to deepen the inquiry.

6a. Design Procedures to Prepare the Materials

Develop clear systems for preparing materials for the classroom meeting to make it easier to transition smoothly.

6b. Design Procedures to Introduce the Problem

You might want to revisit previous play to set the stage for problems children are facing. As you invite children to share the processes, they use their own language to frame the problems they've encountered. In other words, you want to learn the words and phrasing they use to describe their thinking before you introduce a term. Photos or video, as well as the materials from previous play, help children revisit and enter into the conversation. Including a variety of photos from the children's previous play often ignites the thinking of different children.

6c. Design Procedures to Model the Process

Modeling of processes is sometimes a controversial issue for teachers interested in emergent inquiry curriculum. There is a misconception that children lead the curriculum on their own and that modeling takes away the authenticity of the children to construct their own processes with materials and social interactions. On the contrary, children learn from others on a day-to-day basis—at home from a mixed-age blend of family and community members and in school from a diverse grouping of teachers and peers. When you talk with children, you are modeling the use of language and conversational skills in ways that do not coerce children to proceed in one particular way. Modeling a way to use materials in a group setting where open-ended interjections into the conversation are allowed is a wonderful way to present children with an initial approach to working with a particular material.

6d. Design Procedures to Focus the Play

When you design a focused classroom meeting in which the children will break out into working focus groups, it is important to organize the children's thinking around Big Ideas and threads of inquiry (discussed in Chapter 3) to be explored so that the transition to the small groups will run smoothly.

Summary of Guidelines for Planning a Focused Classroom Meeting

1. Observe and Document

   a. Document observations to capture teachers' thinking.

2. Identify a Question or a Problem to Pursue

   a. The problem is developmentally appropriate and of interest to many.

   b. The question or problem stems from children's play and helps them to meta-reflect—think about their thinking, questions, and curiosities.

3. Choose Materials that Will Intrigue and Allow Exploration

   a. Use photos of children's play, their drawings, or any concrete artifacts related to the question or problem you will focus on.

   b. Plan for the materials you will use to document the meeting discussion and activities (camera, written observation record materials, easel for writing what children say in a classroom meeting discussion).

   c. Familiar materials can be explored in new ways, and new materials can be introduced.

4. Design a Setup that Will Capture Dialogue and Invite Exploration

   a. Will children sit in a circle?

   b. Will children gather around work to be studied in a center where the problem is posed (e.g., block center to explore how to build a tall tower or art center to explore how to mix colors)?

   c. Where will you sit in relation to the children and the materials used to explore the problem?

   d. How will your coteacher support you and the children during the meeting time?

5. Form Questions that Will Probe and Extend Children's Thinking

   a. Your intention is to promote open dialogue with the children about their thinking.

6. Design Procedures to

   a. Prepare the materials

   b. Introduce the problem

   c. Model the process

   d. Focus the play

   e. Engage small groups

   f. Facilitate and capture whole group reflections

7. Plan for Follow-Through the Next Day

6e. Design Procedures to Engage Small Groups

Once you have introduced materials, children are generally interested in experimenting with them. Designing small focus groups where all the children in the class have the opportunity to interact with the materials is a great way to meet this challenge.

6f. Design Procedures for Whole Group Reflections

Prepare questions and statements to jump-start the whole group reflections at the close of a focused classroom meeting. You can formulate other questions and ideas as you record your observations of the classroom meeting conversations and interactions, bringing the focus of the thinking back to the original intentions and prompts and including new questions, problems, and insights that emerge from the children. These careful notes can lead to the future design of responsive provocations.

When designing a focused classroom meeting that includes small focus groups, you can plan to reflect immediately following their breakout sessions or in your focused classroom meeting the next day, whichever suits the time frame and the children's ability to stay focused. Children generally want to remain engaged in groups for longer periods when the conversations are related to the work and play that has been particularly meaningful to them.

7. Plan for Follow-Through the Next Day

Use some of the materials and ideas that emerge from the classroom meeting to design follow-up plans for one or more of the few classroom centers where inquiry is focused. Other ongoing interests will continue to be represented in other centers.

Redesign and expand centers as needed to allow for the dual purposes of the inquiry focus and other interests outside the inquiry (see Chapter 1). Sometimes it will be important for a center to focus solely on the unfolding inquiry concepts. For this kind of focused center, you can remove the materials that are not related to that particular inquiry to enable the children to investigate concepts deeply with fewer distractions and interruptions.

Planning a Focused Classroom Meeting: Castle Tower Example

In this example, you'll see how the teachers in one program followed each step of the guidelines in planning for a focused classroom meeting around an inquiry related to castles.

1. Observe and Document

Teachers' documentation data revealed an interest in castles (see Fig. 2.1). Children were seen dramatizing play around castles and building castles in the block center. Teachers observed some children working hard to build a castle with a "tall tower" but having a difficult time. A teacher had previously invited children to draw their block castle structures to help them think about the idea of *tall*. The drawings represented evidence that the children were viewing their block structures from a top view, which suggested they did not understand the concept of tallness, since that understanding would prompt drawings from a side view.

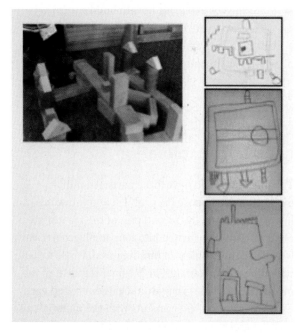

Figure 2.1. Documentation of children's block castle and drawings for the planning of the focused classroom meeting.

2. Identify a Question or a Problem to Pursue

In their review of their written records, photos of the block castle structures, and the children's drawings, the teachers determined there was a developmental interest in castle life and castles. They decided that the problem of how to build a tall castle tower could capture the joint attention and interest of all the children in a whole group meeting.

3. Choose Materials that Will Intrigue Children and Allow Exploration

Teachers gathered the following classroom materials for the initial meeting discussion of the castle towers:

- Pictures of the children's towers, pictures of real towers, and pictures of towers in castle books

- Documentation materials: large pad of paper for capturing ideas, camera for photos, and observation forms for recording children's words and actions

- Materials for exploring how to build tall castle towers in small groups: clay, Unifix cubes, cardboard with slits, and small rectangular unit blocks

4. Design a Setup that Will Capture Dialogue and Invite Exploration

The meeting would have three parts. An initial discussion would pose the problem and introduce materials. During the second part of the meeting, children would be invited into four small groups, each to explore the problem of building a tall castle tower with different materials. For the final segment of the meeting, the whole group would gather around each of the four groups' experiments with the materials so that the group members could share their findings with their peers from other groups.

During the initial discussion the teacher would have a small amount of each material near her at the classroom meeting to discuss and model. For the focused inquiry process, each of the four materials (clay, Unifix cubes, cardboard with slits, and small

blocks) would be placed on a Masonite wood base on the floor in four different areas of the classroom to allow focused exploration.

Similarities of Emergent Inquiry Curriculum to Higher Education

Consider the structure of the emergent inquiry classroom presented in this chapter as similar to the structure of a research university. Each classroom center can be envisioned as a research learning laboratory. The children exploring the materials in each laboratory are gaining expertise that they can eventually share with peers. In academia, research colleagues come together to share their work in progress and their research findings at conferences where they seek feedback from peers that guides their processes forward. The focused classroom meeting can be reinterpreted as a conference where the children, as experts of the learning they have been engaged in, come together to share and obtain feedback to progress further in their inquiry.

5. Form Questions that Will Probe and Extend Children's Thinking

The teachers developed questions for the whole class as well as for the smaller group of children who were engaged in building towers:

1. First, for the entire group:

   a. Are the towers in the pictures of the castles that some of our classroom friends built with blocks as tall as the towers of a castle?

      i. (If yes) Show me where/how.

      ii. (If no) Show me why not.

2. Next, for the children who were building towers:

   a. Tell us how you built your castle tower.

   b. Tell us where you had a problem going tall.

3. Finally, for the entire group:

   a. Would you like to build castle towers?

6. Design Procedures

6a. Design Procedures to Prepare the Materials

In this focused classroom meeting example, the whole group engaged in discussion and then broke out into small focus groups that would each be exploring one problem with different materials. To support this, the coteachers took turns with two roles at snack time. One oversaw the family-style snack where children congregated around three classroom tables. The second teacher organized the materials and related centers for the classroom meeting.

1. *Planning for the classroom meeting gathering spot:* The teacher set out mats for each child around the perimeter of the classroom meeting rug. She placed all the materials needed to introduce a problem—the teacher-initiated provocation materials—near where the teacher would sit. A large chart pad on an easel was also set near the teacher's seat so she could write the dialogue as children converse. She also placed a bin of books in the center. The children had learned that when they finished snack they could move to the rug, take a book from the bin, and read quietly alone or with peers until all were ready for the meeting. Then it was the job of one child to collect the books back into the bin.

2. *Organizing for breakout of small focus groups following the whole group discussion:* While children were eating snack, one teacher organized each breakout area on a different section of floor, each with a drop cloth and its specific materials around which a small group of children could gather to construct castle towers.

   › The Unifix cubes connected together to rise in a linear fashion, which might pose a problem with stability as children tried to build taller. The teacher was interested in presenting challenges for children to face and discuss, so that they could determine which materials were useful for building tall castle towers and which were not when comparing their findings with other the groups'.

   › The rectangular unit blocks were chosen because they were likely to present similar challenges to the large cardboard bricks the children had been using for castle building. The idea of navigating on a smaller scale seemed worthy of exploration to these teachers.

   › Clay was chosen for its ability to be formed into a cylindrical shape using a coil method (below). The teachers intended to show the children how to roll a clay coil and to roll enough for shaping into a few rows with the help of a couple of children during the whole group discussion period.

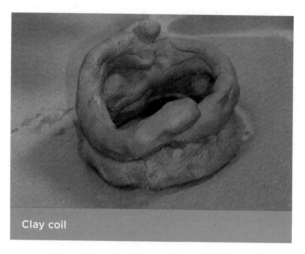
Clay coil

   › Cardboard rectangles with slits (below) allowed for various structural designs, as the walls of the structure can bend with the insertion of each rectangle.

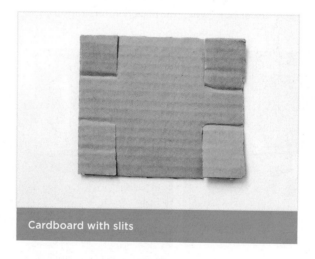
Cardboard with slits

6b. Design Procedures to Introduce the Problem

The teacher showed photos of children's castle towers built with blocks, real castle towers in photographs, and castle towers represented as drawings in books. She then asked the questions she had prepared to begin a dialogue and built on these as needed in response to children's dialogue. She listened to the children share their stories of building castle towers and the ideas about castle towers they were forming by looking at the pictures. As a motivational prompt to hook and maintain their interest for the next steps, the teacher asked if the children would like to build tall castle towers.

6c. Design Procedures to Model the Process

The teacher modeled the processes she was interested in promoting. Using clay, she created a coil and began to build a round structure until she built it as high as three rings of coils. Then she asked for two children to try this process as their peers looked on and provided feedback. When the two children finished, the teacher set these materials aside and brought out one of the other materials. She modeled a process of building with each of three remaining materials, asking one or two children to try each one as others in the whole group gathering observed and learned.

6d. Design Procedures to Focus the Play

The teacher assured the children that they would have time to play with the new materials following their discussion. When the brief demonstration

with each material concluded, the teacher asked the children to make predictions about which materials might work best for building a tall castle tower. Her coteacher recorded the children's predictions on a chart so that the children could see their words represented as symbols on a page, ready to be revisited in upcoming discussions. The children made the following predictions:

- "Unifix cubes can be super straight."

- "Clay can be round, but it is too soft to be a real castle tower."

- "A round castle tower can be made with blocks, because some of those castle towers in the pictures are made with blocks."

- "The block castle tower will be the strongest."

6e. Design Procedures to Engage Small Groups

The teacher introduced the areas where each of the four groups would try to build a castle tower with one of the materials (see the photos below). She let them know that following their explorations they would come back together as a whole class to talk about what each focus group learned about using these materials to build a tall castle tower. Knowing they would be asked to share their discoveries afterward focused their thinking on the processes they would be using. The teacher then

(*From left to right*) Unit block builders; builders with cardboard; Unifix cube builders; builders with clay

From Children's Interests to Children's Thinking

invited children to join their friends at one area, and she moved from group to group to facilitate and to document the building with photos and notes.

6f. Design Procedures for Whole Group Reflections

At the close of play, both teachers gathered the children around the work of one of the building groups, then proceeded to each of the other building groups so children could see and listen as peers shared their experiences with building castle towers. A teacher facilitated dialogue on the similarities and differences with their predictions and the work of other groups, problems encountered, a comparison of the children's castle towers to the ones in the pictures, and children's ideas about the properties and uses of the materials they worked with. These were some of their ideas about the materials:

- "Unifix cubes topple."

- "The space helps the [unit] blocks go taller."

- "[The clay tower] got taller slower, but ours is round like the real castles."

- "We can use the big blocks like [unit blocks]."

7. Plan for Follow-Through the Next Day

During the inquiry into castle towers, the block area was enlarged to accommodate construction related to the long-term project, with plenty of space for children not interested in the inquiry to also build in that center. (This was also true for the art area, which housed two tables. One was always available for the project focus and the other for open-ended exploration of art media.) During the castle tower investigation, the teachers also allowed for the dramatic play area to be dedicated to the children's interpretations of life inside a castle. The teachers prepared for the next day in these ways:

- In the **art area,** papers were prepared, each with a circle drawn in the center. Small clay bricks were placed in little containers, enough so that four children could each have their own. A written prompt stating "Can you make a tall,

round castle tower with these blocks?" was placed at the table to invite children to make a round castle tower. By placing a portion of the bricks on one of the circles on paper, teachers intended for these materials to invite children to build castle towers on these circles. A photo from the classroom meeting is an additional prompt. It pictured the small group that was constructing a castle tower with the unit blocks on a circle made of masking tape on the floor.

Written Prompts

Written prompts guide children to ask what the writing means. This helps to organize the teachers' thinking about the focus of the provocation and serves as an emergent literacy tool for children.

- In the **block area,** a large circle was taped to the floor. The photo of the group working with the unit blocks during the classroom meeting was placed nearby. A couple of large cardboard bricks were set on the masking tape circle to inspire children to build a castle tower.

- In the **manipulative area,** small cubes were provided in a basket in the center of a table along with pictures of castle tower building from the classroom meeting. Circles were drawn onto four pieces of paper placed at each of four seats. These circles were drawn in a size appropriate as a base for constructing castle towers with small cubes.

- Books with images of castles were left on the table in the **art area,** on the floor in the **block area,** and on the table in the **manipulatives area.** Pictures of castles and of children building castle towers in the classroom meeting were posted on the available walls in each of the three provocation centers.

In the days following the castle tower classroom meeting, children successfully built tall, round castle towers with the cardboard bricks (top photo on the following page). They used the method developed by the children in the unit block focus group.

Constructing a tall castle tower

Other children brought small unit blocks into the sand table, using the sand as a structural support to hold the blocks upright. They began to cut out cardboard representations of castles with towers, inspired by the images they saw in the books during the classroom meeting (below).

Using castle thinking in sand table

For Further Reflection and Inquiry

The reflective thinking that occurs when you design focused classroom meetings can ignite a deeper connection to the ongoing inquiry in your classroom. You learn more about children's purposes for play and explorations in these sessions, where you are preparing for them to be the experts and take ownership of their inquiry. These meetings are opportunities to introduce and model use of new materials and strategies for working with materials and peers. Guiding children to think about their thinking helps them to assess their ideas and progress in order to move forward. In the next chapter, a study of bluegrass music is introduced to illustrate the components of a long-term inquiry project.

For deeper reflection on facilitating classroom meetings related to inquiry studies, try these suggestions:

1. Observe in the various learning centers in your classroom to see if you notice a problem or challenge children might be experiencing that you can share with the entire class.

2. As you observe, document the challenges you notice within several learning centers.

3. Document any successes children are experiencing in different areas of the classroom that might be valuable to share with the whole class.

4. Consider what materials you can bring to a classroom meeting to help children further their learning in relation to a challenge, problem, or success you've observed.

5. If your classroom schedule doesn't allow for focused classroom meetings, think of ways to redesign the schedule.

From Children's Interests to Children's Thinking

CHAPTER 3

Identifying Threads of Inquiry, Provocations, and Big Ideas

This chapter introduces a long-term emergent inquiry project centering on the study of bluegrass music. As we briefly described in the Introduction, this class in East Tennessee spent a full school year exploring bluegrass music. Numerous threads of inquiry emerged and were followed and woven together as the teachers worked through many cycles of observing, documenting, interpreting, planning, and reflecting.

Threads of inquiry are the pathways for learning that children follow with the careful facilitation of intentional teachers. They come from both the ideas of children and the musings and observations of teachers. These facets of interest and learning center on Big Ideas, which are content-focused concepts (McLean, Jones, & Shaper 2015) that weave together diverse threads of inquiry. Using threads of inquiry successfully can be a strategy to extend emergent inquiry curricula through an entire year and beyond in one classroom.

Strategies to allow many threads to emerge over time and to link together in a cohesive, meaningful way include finding threads of inquiry, using provocations, weaving threads of inquiry, and finding Big Ideas. In this chapter, you'll learn how to do all of these things. Developing your ability to articulate emerging threads of inquiry and the related Big Ideas is important because it helps you to keep a focus as the inquiry develops over time. You will be looking at the way threads of inquiry and Big Ideas function within the bluegrass study example.

Finding Threads of Inquiry

Teachers using an emergent inquiry curriculum are responsive to children, planning provocations around questions they have developed that challenge the children toward the edges of their own understandings. Teachers identify emerging threads of inquiry during the process of reflecting on their documentation of children's play.

The best indicators of an emerging thread of inquiry are the problems children face during play, the questions they ask, the things they wonder about, and what happens in the moments they show spontaneous curiosity (Forman & Hall 2005). With all the activity in a day's work with children, these key indicators are easily lost if they are not documented by observant teachers (see Chapter 4 for more about the documentation process).

For example, when children in the bluegrass study plucked and strummed the strings of the bluegrass instruments (banjo, guitar, mandolin, fiddle), teachers noted their interest and puzzlement. They observed the children's surprise when they expected the high sound to be on the top string of an instrument and it wasn't. This little bit of a problem led teachers to plan many experiences for studying and discriminating the relationships of high and low sounds with the different bluegrass instruments.

If you find yourself, in your planning, pursuing an idea that is becoming clearer or is tying more content together, you are probably pursuing a thread of inquiry—a pathway for learning. For example, as children began to use the term *band* during the processes of exploring the individual bluegrass and old-time instruments and then referenced themselves as a band during pretend play episodes, teachers realized that the children's ideas went beyond the focus of individual instruments to ideas about groups of instruments and performers. Teachers recognized an emerging thread of inquiry—"What is a band?"—that they could plan around to help children answer this question.

Each thread creates depth and draws both children and teachers into deep pursuit of a problem. Threads are situations in which children want to master skills and challenge their theories. For example, the pursuit of the thread "What is a band?" led children to pretend to form bands and perform with mock instruments, to create scenarios with bands using small figures of band members in a small block area, and to create stages and places for bands to go. They used an extended construction of a city in the block area to explore a new thread of inquiry, "Where do we find bands?" This construction interwove exploration of buildings and structures with the bluegrass study. As a result of these varied experiences, children formalized their thinking to better articulate their ideas about bands. They could specifically state that a typical bluegrass band has five instruments: banjo, fiddle, mandolin, bass, and dobro. They demonstrated developing knowledge of space concepts related to the distances between cities and the size and proportion of stages in relation to cars and roads.

Emergent curriculum is not a go-with-the-flow process. Teachers carefully design provocations (discussed below) that keep the thinking close to the children's current pursuits, while holding the direction of the inquiry close to the children's initial interests, questions, and developing theories. For example, as children listened closely to the words of bluegrass songs and drew their interpretations, there were instances when they diverged from the focus on the songs to draw and talk about rainbows or butterflies. The teachers did not view these conversations as new project opportunities to study rainbows or butterflies. Instead, they paid attention and recognized that overall the children remained deeply engaged in the process of drawing and interpreting the words of the songs. By keeping track of the events of each experience related to the bluegrass study, the teachers' documentation became a critical tool for reflection and planning (Broderick & Hong 2011; Hong 1998). They designed provocations that followed the emerging and spontaneous questions and curiosities of children, intentionally holding the curricular content together within the focus on the bluegrass study.

Using Provocations

Provocations are processes that motivate individuals to act or respond. Educators in Reggio Emilia (Edwards, Gandini, & Forman 2012) introduced the term in relation to the early learning environment. As do many Reggio-inspired educators, we use the term *provocation* to refer to teachers' intentional setup of materials within a learning center to elicit children's responses. The thinking and learning that emerge from the children as they engage with provocations will reveal potential threads of inquiry. Teachers introduce provocations to support the natural tendency of the child's curiosity and intellect to move forward and construct new knowledge. These provocations are designed in the fourth planning phase of the COI and are based on teachers' interpretations and questioning of the meaning of children's engagements they've observed. As you begin to explore how to plan for emergent curriculum in your classroom, you can rely on both teacher-initiated and responsive provocations.

Teacher-Initiated Provocations

Teacher-initiated provocations are based on an interest that teachers believe will engage children's curiosity deeply and support a long period of inquiry (Wien & Halls 2018). You can design teacher-initiated plans around questions or ideas that you want to explore with or about children (McLean, Jones, & Shaper 2015). When you plan around complex concepts over time, the investment of the children will link easily to many early learning standards and developmental goals, not just one. Information about documenting emergent inquiry learning in relation to standards is discussed in Chapter 8. The bluegrass study discussed in this chapter originated through a teacher-initiated provocation.

Creating Teacher-Initiated Provocations

Sometimes you will have questions in mind before the school year starts. These may come to arise as you reflect on

- Children's processes from a previous year

- Your ideas about children's interests, based on your professional expertise

- Your questions about your own teaching practice

- A passion of yours, such as an interest in friendships or storytelling

- The culture of your classroom as the students begin to form a community

Educators in Reggio Emilia note that their curriculum is particular to their culture and cannot be replicated. If you are inspired by their practices, identify cultural aspects of your setting for possible curricular focus, whether it is the makeup of children and families in your classroom or a cultural phenomenon in your locale, such as the bluegrass music in Appalachia or the influence of the ocean on coastal communities.

The choice of an emergent curriculum focus is very particular to the culture and experiences of the children and families, teachers, and program. At one school, the development of painting among children throughout all classrooms, from toddlers to 4s and 5s, became the emergent curriculum interest. The focus of this yearlong study generated from a discovery among teachers that children ages 4 and 5 were generally painting with the same broad gestural brush stroke techniques that toddlers employed. This led the teachers to wonder what they would notice about the differences in the approaches of children ages 2, 3, 4, or 5 by paying closer attention to the painting processes at each age level throughout the preschool. They questioned how they might support children's development with painting and what techniques they might need to research to be able to support a broader range of skill development at each age level than was previously provided.

A Teacher-Initiated Provocation Example from the Bluegrass Study

The bluegrass study began with a teacher-initiated provocation in which teachers invited a student of bluegrass music to perform for the children with one of her band members. The teachers' plan was based on their ideas about how they incorporated music into their classroom and whether they could expand children's interest and awareness of music through an exploration of the local culture of bluegrass music and the possible connections with the children's own lives. This excerpt from their early documentation presents the rationale for their provocation:

The children are naturally musical and interested in all different kinds of music. We introduce all types of music and observe that music inspires children to experiment with different types of movement. Music is used for morning greeting, celebrations, transitions from one activity to another, and constructive playtime. Because we live in a music-rich area of the country (located in East Tennessee) children have lots of music opportunities available to them. We chose bluegrass music as a focus for discovery to link children's learning to this culture and region.

Responsive Provocations

In contrast to teacher-initiated provocations, responsive provocations are the interventions you design that are responsive to children's interests and pursuits observed during child-initiated play. They are the plans formed as a result of synthesizing the many ideas you generate about children's theories and ways to plan curriculum that can help children explore their ideas more deeply. As you read through this book, you will learn how teachers' plans for curriculum are framed around questions they reflect on. They carefully revise their questions into designs for exploration that most closely align with the children's diverse theories of the phenomena they are investigating. In the bluegrass study illustrated in this chapter, you will see examples of teacher-initiated provocations as well as responsive provocations.

As noted previously, many emergent inquiry teachers don't have an emergent curriculum focus in mind at the start of the year. These teachers set up their classrooms with basic learning center materials that are typical of preschool classrooms, such as daily living, manipulatives, blocks, sand and water, art, and literacy. They organize a flexible daily schedule that incorporates a strong focus on long periods of open-ended and uninterrupted constructive play and allows time for classroom meetings with the whole group and small groups as well as for snack, nap time, and outdoor play.

Without an emergent curriculum focus at the start of the school year, teachers observe the children interacting in each area and document carefully to determine a topic for exploration that responds to the interests, questions, and challenges of the children as they interact with the environment and respond to daily life at school. These teachers choose a particular focus from among the many interests and challenges they observe because they are aware that their content choice will offer children a wide range of opportunities to explore deeply with many media over a long-term process.

A Responsive Provocation Example from the Bluegrass Study

Documentation of children listening to two performers of bluegrass music revealed that children were listening carefully to the words in the songs.

> "Are you talking about a Rocky Top story?" asks Jason. "I think it's a mountain," says Jason, and he adds, "Tennessee." "We live in Tennessee," says Chloe. Mary relates Rocky Top to another song about a sense of place when she says, "I know 'This Land Is Your Land.'"

In response to children's interest in the words of the songs, teachers designed a provocation in which children could reflect on the meanings of the words in certain songs. With a CD of old-time music playing, the children listened with interest to the many songs, including the well-known tunes "Down in the Valley"

and "Keep on the Sunny Side." Musicians visited the classroom (below) and sang "Freight Train," a song they wrote. They left a CD of their music for the children to listen to. Teachers set out paper and colored pencils as an invitation to draw, and they encouraged children to listen for the words they knew in each bluegrass song and use their drawings to tell the story they heard in the music. Jimmy related to the word "valley" by drawing a picture of hills and valleys. His teachers thought his drawing of a sidewalk leading to the hills and valleys was his response to the words "taking a journey."

Two musicians sing and play a bluegrass song on their guitars in a concert-like setting, with performers facing the children, in an initial teacher provocation to gauge children's interest in this music as an inquiry focus.

Julie drew a picture of a scene with a bright sun and flowers to represent the "sunny side of life," and she drew another scene of a "dark stormy side" with a dying tree and the edge of the earth (top image, following page). She said, "The tree is sick." This was a symbolic and poetic representation of the lyrics. She was describing elements of the world, real and imagined, as symbols for the expressions of happiness and sadness interpreted from the song. Chloe interpreted "Keep on the Sunny Side" with a multicolored sun, a train track, a train, and a tunnel that wrapped over the sun (bottom image, following page). The sun was made using concentric circles and a darkened spot in the middle. The train was made of lines that formed an intersection in the middle. "I was thinking about the freight train," she said. "That's the sunshine."

Julie draws a bright sun and a darker stormy image to represent the story she hears in "Keep on the Sunny Side."

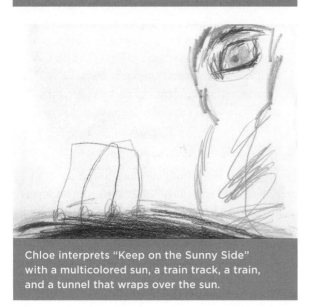

Chloe interprets "Keep on the Sunny Side" with a multicolored sun, a train track, a train, and a tunnel that wraps over the sun.

Ideas for Generating Provocations

Some methods for generating provocations are discussed in the other chapters that describe setting up an emergent inquiry classroom at the start of the year, as well as how to document, interpret, and plan from your observations of children. As an initial practice, you can allow for long, uninterrupted constructive play and document your observations. Here are just a few suggestions for determining a provocation:

- Identify cultural phenomena in your area that
  - › Are familiar to children in your classroom and their families
  - › Will interest children over a long period of time

- Document your observations of children during uninterrupted play to
  - › Learn their strong interests
  - › Learn something they know that surprises you and might guide you to plan for ways to extend through a responsive provocation

Weaving the Threads of Inquiry

The provocations you initiate or design in response to children can generate new lines of thinking. Some provocations will be focused on the small core group around which the inquiry begins, and others will draw the interest of other small core groups. Weaving threads of inquiry is the process of allowing several threads to coexist and blend in a curricular trajectory. Below is a sampling of several threads of inquiry that emerged within the bluegrass study. (See Tables 3.1–3.3 on pages 38–40 for a more comprehensive but not exhaustive list of threads.)

- **Familiar musical instruments.** A thread developed about how instruments, particularly those associated with bluegrass music, work and what sounds they make. Some of the learning within this thread related to science and music standards. Children learned to discriminate the sounds of the different instruments, distinguishing a mandolin from a dobro, a banjo, a guitar, or a fiddle in recordings. They developed an understanding of how the thickness of an instrument's string influences pitch, and they improved their ability to identify different music genres, such as classical, jazz, and folk.

- **Stories and meanings behind song lyrics.** This thread emerged from documentation of the children's first experiences with listening to the language of the bluegrass songs. Children engaged in art and literacy learning by using a variety of art media to draw and symbolize their understandings of the meaning in the songs they heard. Through conversations while drawing and painting, children developed communication and receptive language skills as they shared ideas and showed respect for the perspectives of friends.

- **What is a band?** As children watched video performances of bluegrass and old-time bands, many identified the concept of a band with their local culture. Several children told teachers that they had family members who performed in bands, played instruments, and played bluegrass music on the radio in the car and at home. Children also mentioned that they had been to performances of regional music. While teachers were learning about children's social experiences with bluegrass music, the children were strengthening their appreciation of and relationship with their culture through this study.

- **What is a performance?** In a small block area with figures of five bluegrass band members similar to paper dolls, children created small block structures they referred to as the stages on which these figures performed, the buses that carried the musicians to hotel structures, and the beds in which the band members slept (photo at right). This spontaneous play helped teachers understand what the children knew about band performances and touring, which led the teachers to set up a stage in the classroom with mock bluegrass instruments (photo at right on following page). This sort of play provided another avenue for social and cultural learning. Children brought in ideas about bands that they talked about at home with family members who had traveled in bands and shared this knowledge with others. Some of their conversations focused on the relationship of a band to an audience. When children arranged several chairs in a row facing the classroom stage one day, the teachers realized there was opportunity to engage in conversations about the role of the audience. Children learned that people not only listen to the performers, they also dance, and in their regional tradition the dancing is flatfooting.

- **We can write and read music.** When a child wrote a string of words using invented spelling with three strings of horizontal lines below and sang from her words while strumming a child-size

In this teacher-initiated provocation, children reveal what they know about performing and touring as they use small blocks to construct stages, buses, and hotels for the "band members."

guitar, she initiated a thread of inquiry focusing on music notation (photo at top left on following page). Teachers responded by designing a center for writing music notations that included a set of colored handbells with correlating colored markers (photo at bottom left on following page). By correlating marks to sounds of bells, children learned that marks hold meaning and that others could read what they write and play along with the handbells. Eventually, teachers added concert bells, which look like a xylophone, to the center using colored tape correlating this instrument's keys with the handbell set. Thus, children learned that they could read their notations and play along with two instruments. This early literacy experience captured the children's interest for several months. They were typically organizing patterns of colors more than of sound, which also relates to early math.

The many threads within the bluegrass study overlapped and continued simultaneously over many months, from October to May. There was a back-and-forth dynamic of teacher-initiated and child-initiated processes within the larger curricular focus as teachers observed, documented, and reflected on

- When to allow the children to lead the inquiry independent of teacher intervention

- When to generate a provocation to challenge children to engage in new thinking as they followed a thread of inquiry

From Children's Interests to Children's Thinking

A child writes and then reads her music notation, "Eh Day La La La La/Eh Day La La La La," as she pretends to play the mock instrument on the classroom stage. In response, teachers design a center where children can write music they can then read and sing.

■ When to share information about a thread of inquiry to inform the whole class and to help children make connections between the diverse threads of inquiry that were being explored

Figure 3.1 illustrates the three Big Ideas of the bluegrass study and the sequence of many of the emerging threads in the investigation. Each thread is coded with a different color. In the figure, a circle represents focused classroom meetings initiated and organized by the teacher to bring the thinking of one small group of children to the whole class. A rectangle represents ongoing small core group work. This work was often spontaneous and child initiated, but it may have also been the direct result of responsive or teacher-initiated provocations intentionally designed to invite children to explore and investigate. It was within the child-initiated activities that the threads of inquiry progressed; however, it was through the teacher-initiated focused classroom

Figure 3.1. Big Ideas and threads of inquiry in the bluegrass study. The Big Ideas are noted at the top of each thread, and each thread is represented by a different color. Circles represent whole group meetings with teacher-initiated processes. Rectangles represent child-initiated processes that occurred spontaneously in learning centers where bluegrass study materials were provided through teachers' responsive provocations.

The Context of Bluegrass Music

Exploring the audience, where the band is found in the community, dancing as an audience, and the stage setting and performers

Music Notation

Playing from the notations we write

Music Notation

Playing music for one instrument on another instrument

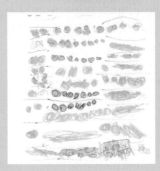

meetings that the threads most effectively interacted and fed one another. Through these planned and focused classroom meetings, teachers provided children the opportunities to weave together the threads they were pursuing independently in their small group experiences.

In any inquiry, each thread can be explored over a long period with a variety of materials and in a variety of settings within the classroom. For example, the thread of inquiry on music notation began with children using markers to represent the individual notes of a set of handbells. The thread continued over a long period of time, with children eventually using pastels and watercolors to represent the sound of the handbells and a set of concert bells. This work started in the writing center where children linked the idea of writing music to writing with meaning. The music notation work eventually moved out of the writing area nearer to the music stage, so children could write their music and then play it. The writing area then became free for children to write stories about the band characters they played with in the block center.

Finding Big Ideas

A Big Idea is a core framework that links together several emerging threads of inquiry (Chaille 2008). Curriculum content can be organized into very broad and inclusive categories, for example "art as language" and "patterns around us," that experts in content fields know and use (McLean, Jones, & Shaper 2015). Some early childhood teachers will be aware of the Big Ideas in certain fields. A Big Idea structures content as a network of concepts for possible study and exploration. A thread of inquiry can refer to a focus on a particular concept in this network of concepts.

While threads exist within children's play, Big Ideas become apparent as you observe and reflect on children's play over time. During observation and planning, you can identify Big Ideas that are approachable through the children's play and that are worth investigating. You will appropriately time new provocations in response to the threads you recognize within the current play that you've documented on the COI forms, which will be discussed in the next several chapters. These threads can exist simultaneously or follow one another within the overall course of the curriculum, as long as they remain close to the children's diverse interests and theories.

Teacher as Researcher

When you find children interested in content you aren't familiar with, you can research information about the concepts related to the topic to assist you in guiding in-depth inquiry with children. Keep in mind that your goal will be to help children follow their own questions related to the concepts you are all studying. Teachers working with emergent inquiry value learning along with children and enjoy the role of teacher researcher. You can explore by

- Contacting experts on the topic

- Locating books in the library

- Reading about the topic in education journals online

Here are some examples of Big Ideas with related threads of inquiry:

- Art as a language: Using many art materials to (1) learn the properties of the materials, (2) communicate stories, and (3) show ideas about how things work (machines, wind, rain)

- The relationship between light and shadow: Using different light sources in natural and controlled environments, in relation to children and objects to explore (1) movement of shadows, (2) disappearance of shadows, and (3) variations in proportion and size of shadows

- Patterns around us: Using observation to (1) discover the unique organization of flower petals, (2) identify the structure of the veins of leaves and limbs of trees, (3) become aware of the symmetrical and asymmetrical relationships of windows to doors in buildings, and (4) discover similarities and differences in the pattern of bricks or stones in a wall

From Children's Interests to Children's Thinking

We recommend planning long-term emergent inquiry curriculum around Big Ideas and threads of inquiry, which will incorporate the interests and skills you are observing among children in your classroom. You will then want to create a consistent schedule, biweekly or every few weeks, for checking the learning you are observing against the early learning standards of your state and your program. In this way, when you discover standards that may not be addressed in the curriculum, you can consider ways to incorporate them in ways that align with the long-term inquiry within your classroom.

In the bluegrass study, teachers' careful reflection on their documentation of child observations identified three Big Ideas of the ways children were most engaged through the evolution of the bluegrass study:

1. The **science of music** was identified as a Big Idea based on the deep interest children demonstrated in continually seeking to listen to and identify the instruments specific to bluegrass music. Therefore, many responsive provocations and teacher-initiated provocations centered on this Big Idea.

You will often discover two overarching curricular structures that can emerge, engage children, and be managed simultaneously within an emergent inquiry curriculum classroom. Consider, for example, a building and structures exploration that developed alongside the bluegrass study. Children explored roads, bridges, cities, and communities, eventually using small blocks to creat the stages where bluegrass musicians perform, the hotels where they sleep, and the buses they travel in, all within the children's city structures.

2. The **context of bluegrass music** was identified as a Big Idea based on documentation of children's conversations about family members who played in bands, the meanings of the songs they listened to, and the ways children began to construct band stages in the block area.

3. **Music notation** was identified as a Big Idea following the process of one child writing a song she could sing. This inspired teachers to design a music-writing center as a responsive provocation, and children were engaged in writing music they could read and play for many months.

Tables 3.1–3.3 show how long it took for the many threads of inquiry to emerge and continue within the framework of each of the three Big Ideas in the bluegrass study.

Table 3.1. The Science of Music (October 8 Through January 7)

BIG IDEA: THE SCIENCE OF MUSIC		
Dates	**Teacher-Initiated Threads**	**Child-Initiated Threads**
Oct. 8	**Learning bluegrass and old-time instruments.** Inviting musicians to play a bluegrass and old-time music concert	
Oct. 8	**The science of sound.** Representing tempo	Representing tempo in response to teacher
Oct. 8		Representing pitch by noticing high and low sounds on each instrument during first exploration
Oct. 8–13	**Learning bluegrass and old-time instruments.** Inviting children to draw images of themselves as musicians playing bluegrass and old-time instruments	
Oct. 13	**The science of sound.** Playing bluegrass and old-time instruments with intentional questions about pitch	
Oct. 15	**Learning bluegrass and old-time instruments.** Introducing the instruments	
Oct. 15	**The science of sound.** Creating photo representations to scale of each bluegrass instrument for children to use in games as cards to identify the specific instruments by name	
Oct. 15–mid-Nov.		Identifying the bluegrass and old-time instruments with cards representing each
Oct. 17–19	**The science of sound.** Using photo representations of bluegrass instruments to scale to play a game about which one has a higher or lower sound	
Oct. 15–Dec. 17		Exploring high and low on a banjo continues over a period of months
Oct. 22	**The science of sound.** Discriminating the sounds of each bluegrass instrument using CD recording of bluegrass band members' breakout sessions and photo representations of bluegrass instruments children choose when they hear the instrument on the CD	Discrimination of sound of each bluegrass instrument continues for a period of time
Nov. 10 into Dec.	**The science of sound.** Exploring individual bluegrass instruments over time	Noticing that a violin is a fiddle in bluegrass
Dec.	**The science of sound.** Providing many materials to study the quality of sound and how sounds are made within the context of a box and strings (large water jug, boxes, cans, wires, guitar strings, wooden pegs, screws, dowels, blocks)	Representing tempo through the experience of bowing the fiddle slow and fast
Jan. 7	**Stories and meanings behind song lyrics.** Inviting children to draw images of themselves as musicians playing bluegrass instruments	

Table 3.2. The Context of Bluegrass Music (October 22 Through Early February)

BIG IDEA: THE CONTEXT OF BLUEGRASS AND OLD-TIME MUSIC		
Dates	**Teacher-Initiated Threads**	**Child-Initiated Threads**
Oct. 22–29	**Representing the meaning of the songs.** Children are invited to draw what they hear, the story of the song.	**Representing the meaning of the songs** through drawing.
Nov. 18–27		Children act out the stories they draw.
Nov. 3 into Feb.	**What is a band?** Teachers create a small set of blocks with images of bluegrass band members taped onto them, each playing his or her instrument. These are set up on a small block table near the writing area.	**What is a band?** Children create a stage for the figures in the small block area, showing that they understand that bluegrass and old-time music are performed on a stage.
Nov. 3 into Feb.	**What is a band?** Teachers write the stories of the block play with children, supporting literacy skills while learning more about children's social and cultural knowledge of bluegrass and old-time music.	**What is a band?** Children use the small block area for dramatic play and provide answers to the many questions about where they find bands and what a band is; they show us that they have thought about how bands travel to a hotel and play in the park, etc.
Nov. 19	**What is a band/performance?** Teachers respond to children's small block play in which stages are created and bands are talked about. They play a video of bluegrass bands performing, projecting it on a wall in the studio arts room.	**What is a band?** Children show they think that all the bluegrass and old-time instruments are part of a band when they are played by a group.
Nov. 23 into Feb.	**Where do we find bands? Tie-in to context of local community experience and ideas about city.** Teachers ask children where they would hear music in the city and what a stage is.	
Early Jan.	**What is a band/stage/performance?** Teachers create a stage where they set out teacher-created bluegrass instruments (photocopies on wood to scale of children) and microphones.	**What is a band/stage/performance?** Children say they need a special area for their stage, microphones, and instruments. Children pretend to play the pretend instruments and sing. Children stop singing and listen when CD is played; then belt out the song once CD stops playing (they are listening intently). Children set up chairs in front of the stage for the audience.
Early Feb.	**Bluegrass music performance.** Teachers visit Carter Fold (home and stage center of the Carter family musicians) to videotape the band on stage, the seated audience, and the dancing audience. Teachers play video for children.	Children are inspired to dance in response to the Carter Fold video.

Table 3.3. Music Notation (March 2 Through May)

BIG IDEA: MUSIC NOTATION		
Dates	**Teacher-Initiated Threads**	**Child-initiated Threads**
Mar. 2		**We can write and read music.** Child goes to writing center and writes lines across a page with letters above them. She takes this paper over to the stage, asks her teacher to hold it while she reads it, then sings and strums the real child-size guitar. Her invented spelling is readable as "E DE La La La La."
Mar. 3	**We can write and read music.** Teachers invite children to write music. They bring out a colored handbell set and a set of markers correlated to the bell colors. **We can write and read music.** Teachers invite this group of three children to show the entire class how to play the bells when reading their music notations.	**We can write and read music.** Children write music modeled after the first example, with strings of letters and lines. **We can write and read music.** One child begins to draw a literal depiction of the bells; she sees her friend represent a bell sound with a circle, and changes strategies to create a string of symbols that are colored circles instead of letters across the page; two other children model their notations after this approach in this and the next couple of notation sessions.
Mid-Mar. into May	**How to read and play from music notation.** In whole class meetings, teachers invite children to show peers how to read and play their music notation. Teachers also introduce a concert bell instrument to add to the handbell set that children will use to play their music.	**How to read and play from music notation.** Many more children take an interest in writing music and playing the bells while reading their friends' notations.
Apr.–May	**How to write, read, and interpret music notation.** Teachers introduce new colored materials to draw notations, such as pastels.	**How to write, read, and interpret music notation.** Diverse meanings emerge for the notations—a big circle means a long sound and a small circle means a short sound; an orange circle around a green one means to play both bells at the same time. The ability to rub and create various textures encourages new meanings for the notations, such as fuzzy lines representing soft sounds.

From Children's Interests to Children's Thinking

For Further Reflection and Inquiry

Through the story of the bluegrass music study, you have learned about teacher-initiated and responsive provocations used to draw out children's thinking. These provocations are then organized as threads of inquiry. In the bluegrass music study, the diverse threads of inquiry were accessible to a wide range of children, providing opportunities for engagement in the block center, the music writing center, centers for dramatic play with small band figures, the music stage, and the art center. Children's actions, such as creating a music-performing stage with small blocks in response to stories of family members or friends who played bluegrass instruments in bands, provided information about their connection to music at home and inspired new learning. The initial writing and playing of music by one child was influenced by her father's writing of music at home and led teachers to invite the father to play for the class one day. Anji, a young child from China who was receptive to spoken English during the fall of the year but did not speak it consistently, was the first to sing to the linear progression of invented notes of her music notation.

The concept of Big Ideas was introduced in this chapter as a framework of concepts that weave together many threads of inquiry. Teachers identified three Big Ideas through their consistent reflection on the many developing threads in the bluegrass study. They continually assessed the connection of emerging threads to these three Big Ideas.

The bluegrass study's success sprang from many elements. The learning experiences were relevant to children's daily lives and engaged them on an intellectual level. The long-term inquiry connected children to the community in which they live, where bluegrass and old-time music are prevalent on the radio and in weekly performances on the streets of the three cities within the region. Teachers' careful documentation of the interactions among children and teachers guided the teacher-initiated and responsive curriculum, which allowed teachers to intentionally plan in relation to the individual abilities and knowledge of children from diverse family backgrounds. You will begin your own journey with observing intentionally and documenting the details, discussed in Chapter 4.

For deeper reflection on identifying threads of inquiry, provocations, and Big Ideas, try these suggestions:

1. Think back and see if you can recall spontaneous play that children seem to repeat, using the same language and ideas. List the variations of this play that you remember and try to write what you think might be a Big Idea that can weave these play experiences together.

2. Encourage children to participate in a conversation that they guide about a topic that holds great interest to them. Listen closely, document the many details within the conversation, and later reflect on which details might be developed into distinct threads of inquiry.

CHAPTER 4
Observing with Intention

In the many hours that teachers spend observing children, they are inspired and informed by children's wisdom and curiosity. They seek ways to support and strengthen children's inquisitive nature. This interest in children's own inquiry is what leads teachers toward an emergent curriculum. They want to plan for engaging, meaningful short- and long-term projects that are generated from observations of children's play (Forman & Hall 2005; Gandini & Goldhaber 2001). The question of how to design curriculum that influences the forward movement of children's play and learning is huge for teachers who are expected to match their observations to developmental competencies and incremental progressions for learning content, checking to be sure children are developing according to developmental milestones. This chapter focuses on observing children with the intention of designing emergent inquiry curriculum. It offers you a first step for planning from your observations of children's natural play.

A teacher pays close attention to and documents the details of the children's play she observes.

Observing to Interpret the Meaning in Children's Play

In your emergent inquiry classroom, the forward movement of your curriculum depends on the ways you organize—the environment, spaces, time, materials, and interactions—to be responsive to children's thinking. A first step in being responsive to children is to observe through play's natural twists and turns, probing for children's interests, needs, and thinking and looking for significant moments (e.g., conflicts, questions, misconceptions) that will help you interpret what the play means to the children. Any shift in the provision or preparation of materials, questions posed, or teacher–child interactions intended to guide children's inquiry and be responsive to children's purposes must be in relation to an understanding of the children's perspectives and intentions—their thinking. Yet thinking cannot be observed. It can only be inferred through interpretation, a subjective process that draws on your thinking and your ideas about the meaning of children's behaviors. To plan in relation to children's thinking, you will develop interpretations from your intentional observation records.

Working with observations in a subjective manner may be new to you. Many teacher-training programs teach students to observe as a way of objectively assessing for developmental milestones using a variety of checklists and anecdotes and discourage subjectively interpreting children's play.

Taking the perspective of active children who do not often state what they think or the reasons behind their actions is complex (Carter 2018). It involves the development of empathy and being open to the child's experiences. Interpreting the thinking behind

From Children's Interests to Children's Thinking

children's play relies on precise observation records for revisiting and interpreting, as discussed in this chapter. Teachers new to emergent inquiry often say they feel awkward with interpreting the meaning of children's play because they have been told to not be subjective. Learning to interpret children's thinking feels foreign. According to Meg, a teacher,

> We learn about these standardized measures for why we held expectations for children and then we make documentation fit that. We don't capture what children are doing and then learn about standardized tools that will explain what we're seeing. It's completely backwards.

A detailed observation record completed for emergent inquiry planning can be assessed for children's development in addition to children's thinking. Consider the following brief example taken from a longer observation record of a group of four children playing outdoors and pretending to be dinosaurs.

> Darren runs around and around, following a teacher. When the teacher helps another student, Darren goes over to the fence and begins to shake it. The teacher asks him, "Do you want to go over to play with your friends?" Darren looks at the teacher, then goes over to where Jon is playing. He picks up some mulch, puts it on a tree stump, and pretends to eat it. Then he begins yelling. Jon yells back unclearly. Darren grabs Jon's hand. Jon grabs back.

The teacher could assess that Darren's gross motor skills are on target for his age, that he demonstrates cognitive skills by following the teacher's suggestion, and that he is yelling around other children, which might reveal a need to further observe his social interaction skills. With guidance on how to interpret the meaning of the children's play, however, this teacher may discover that Darren intentionally follows the teacher, perhaps to engage her attention at some point, and that he successfully enters play with peers by yelling like a dinosaur, an act that the other children embrace because he fills a role in their dramatic play scenario in which they are pretending to be dinosaurs.

She may also decide to observe both children for longer periods of time to see if their interest is truly tied to dinosaur enactments or the idea of being strong and powerful, among many other possibilities she may discover from observing their play.

We recommend that you decide where to observe and record based on play that appears meaningful, where children are focused and engaged. Initially, interpret for the meaning to children and then review at a later time to document how the play addresses development. Chapter 8 discusses recording the ways emergent inquiry meets early learning standards.

The Significance of Teachers' Thinking to Emergent Curriculum Planning

Teachers can only observe what children do and say, noticing the details surrounding a child's actions and words. What children are doing, noticing, or saying provides insight into the children's goals, their strategies, and their theories about the phenomena that are capturing their attention at the moment (Carter 2018; Curtis 2017; Forman & Hall 2005). You cannot see what children are thinking. Your interpretations are *your* ideas. They are *your* thinking about children's thinking. They are working hypotheses. Emergent inquiry curriculum values your thinking because it is up to you to determine just what to observe, record, and interpret as the basis for planning for simple adjustments to the environment to challenge the children to new levels of learning in the context of the play and inquiry they are pursuing.

Consider focusing your observations on the children who stay involved within an activity over a long period of time, when the processes engage their interests, their intellect, and their social needs. You will want to observe these children to learn more about the meaning of their play, because they do not necessarily talk about their decisions about their play pursuits, and they may not be aware of how to communicate the reasoning behind the actions of their play.

How Observation Informs Teacher Facilitation

Thoughtful modification based on your observations can guide play along its natural course, pull children back to something that no longer sustains their interest, or draw them on to another situation if that will offer materials or people to help address their need (Curtis 2017).

For example, teachers in one classroom noticed several 3-year-old children continually circling throughout their classroom holding cars that they were intentionally pretending to be moving or driving. The teachers chose to design a responsive provocation and modify the learning environment to extend the thinking behind these actions. To stay close to children's interests and intentions for driving moving vehicles, teachers taped a large sheet of paper onto a long table with black paint on a nearby palette. Their idea was that the black paint would track the movement of the vehicles to focus the children's thinking on the results of their actions. Children were invited to dip the wheels of their cars into the black paint and then run the wheels on the paper's surface. On this paper surface, children continued to move the cars in a circular direction, creating a black path that connected their thinking about the cars' movements to the surface of a road. These painted paths became part of a structure for the eventual development of a city with roads, parking lots, and representations of buildings from children's own experiences.

Emergent inquiry curriculum, like this extended road and city project, develops from any shifts with the materials or the social setting that influence the movement and complexity of children's play. Just as curriculum can guide inquiry further, it can also keep children from moving along to further their pursuits if the teacher doesn't observe carefully and interpret their goals. These teachers didn't plan a modification until observing the children for quite a long time to allow children to shift their actions of circling vehicles around the classroom toward new directions for play and thinking. Based on the long-term engagement with these vehicles, teachers were not clear that children were furthering their learning and believed that the provocation with paint would capture children's interests and extend their thinking. The teachers' careful observation and interpretation led the children to explore their thinking from a new perspective.

Through this emergent inquiry process, the teachers documented many developmental domains of learning for the children's portfolios, including these:

- Physical science: acting on objects to produce desired effects and to observe the reactions

- Symbolic development: representing ideas and feelings through movement, conversation, construction, and pretend play

- Language: developing new vocabulary related to roads, paint, community, and so on while developing conversational skills

Developing a practice of carefully recording and interpreting observations is necessary for initiating any emergent inquiry curricula planning. Teachers are not always clear on what to record. The COI Observation Record is a form developed to bridge teachers' recorded observations of children with their initial interpretations.

The COI Observation Record Form
What to Document

Planning for emergent inquiry curriculum begins when you decide to notice that the actions and words of children are significant for understanding their interests, needs, and thinking. The COI Observation Record is where you record the children's actions and words using written running records with photographs, or video that you transcribe. You can locate the form in Appendix 1. In the written records, children's actions are recorded as objective descriptions and are differentiated from children's spoken words by enclosing actions in parentheses, a technique that helps you to quickly distinguish actions and words when rereading. When using video, you will generally develop written records from the sections of video that you think will be most useful for future planning, and you will record the time stamp for the video frames you describe.

Teachers new to documenting play generally focus tightly on developmental behaviors, personality traits, probable developmental limits, or breakthroughs. Recording children's ability to cut with scissors will assist in planning for skill development, but not for children's inquiry. Instead, pay attention to how the children are thinking, imagining their purposes as you observe their play develop through a series of events. Seek to document episodes that you think represent rich content and experiences that children will want to continue to explore. Follow children as they pursue a specific idea in their play. If the play moves from one place to another, move with the children so you can record the details of the play if they are meaningfully linked to the earlier observations. You might even follow the play from one day to the next. To observe more closely, it's wise to develop a plan with a coteacher so one of you can focus on observing the inquiry while the other supports children throughout the classroom. Some programs are able to hire an extra teacher or invite parents, grandparents, and senior community members to volunteer as supports when in-depth documentation is needed.

If not many children respond to the topic or the observed play doesn't continue to be visible during the conversation or play over several days, then you have choices. Continue to look for play that seems to capture children's attention over a longer period. Create a provocation, a learning opportunity, that might enlist the focus of a group of children around this same topic or another topic discovered through observing in order to learn more about children's thinking on the topic.

From this evidentiary record—the COI Observation Record form—you will build diverse interpretations of what the play is about and use these as the basis for curricular plans to extend the thinking, knowledge, and experiences of the children.

Memos

Early in the documentation process, keep your thinking as open and divergent as possible. Teachers developing emergent inquiry curriculum like to brainstorm many possible directions for the curriculum to unfold, which is a divergent thinking process. It is also a feature of creative thinking. Thinking carefully about the various ways children are thinking within the play you document prepares you for this brainstorming process, which you will explore in depth in Chapter 6.

Early on, what is most important for building a curriculum is for you to correlate your observation records to your immediate thinking (best guesses) about what children know, think, and mean. You will note this initial thinking in the memo section of the COI Observation Record form. These subjective interpretations and questions link your observation records to children's thinking and will be useful to revisit during a deeper interpretation process, presented in Chapter 5. Generally, teachers' questions are more important than their answers for building a curriculum that follows and extends the children's thinking and knowledge. Many teachers also include their own drawings of children's constructions or processes as a way of reflecting on what is observed.

Staying Open and Divergent with Memos

Figure 4.1 is an example of a section from a COI Observation Record in which the teacher has made clear choices as to what to document, carefully capturing in great detail the actions and words of children playing in the block area. Her memos focus on her thinking about what the children are thinking. These interpretations reveal many divergent lines of thinking that could be developed into several explorations that will link together meaningfully as threads of inquiry. For example, in three of her memos the teacher states that children are thinking about the parts of a road, that roads lead to different places, and that roads are different shapes.

The ideas recorded in color were later identified by the teacher and her coteacher when revisiting the documentation during an in-depth planning session using the next two COI planning forms. Each topic noted in color is a thread of inquiry for which the teachers eventually designed learning provocations over the course of many months in this long-term investigation. Thus, the content from this play extended into multiple learning opportunities over many months of the school year. The process of revisiting observation records for in-depth planning is discussed in Chapters 5 and 6.

Names	Descriptions	Memos	
Ben	These are the marks on the road. They are there to make it look like a road. (Draws the marks that are in the middle of a road)	Here they are thinking about the different parts of a road	Road structures
Ben	Roads help the cars drive so they don't have to drive on the grass. (Draws straight lines for his road)		
Zada	I'm drawing my house and my road. There is a lot of traffic at my house. (Draws her idea of her house)		
Kevin	I'm drawing a city. These are lots of buildings in a city. (Points to our pictures of cities)		
Jolene	My road goes to Zada's house. (Points to her friend Zada)	They realize that roads lead to different places.	
Ben	Roads are for cars so they can go to different houses. They have stoplights and red means stop, yellow means slow down, and green means go. Traffic lights tell cars what to do so they won't crash.	This child understands the concept of traffic lights.	**Purpose of roads.** Traffic lights and roads lend order to their world.
Zada	My road goes to Jolene's house. (Points to Jolene)		
Jolene	My road has a bridge that goes over it because I live in Watauga, Tennessee. (Draws a shape for her bridge)	They are thinking about the different structures of roads.	
Ben	Maybe roads to go banks or grocery stores.	They are again realizing that roads lead to different places.	
Jolene	We have a river that goes to my house and a bridge that we drive on. (Points to where her bridge is)		
Ben	If there weren't any roads, we would have to take a jet because they don't need roads. (Continues to draw his city)	Here they are thinking about the different types of transportation.	Diverse transportation
Kevin	This road is going to an airport. (Continues to draw his roads)		
Kevin	If there were no lines on roads, cars wouldn't know where to turn. (Adds lines to his roads he has drawn)	This child is thinking about the different purposes of roads.	
Zada	My roads are straight. (Draws straight lines)	This shows that the children realize roads are different shapes and go in different directions.	Direction
Jolene	My roads are curvy. (Makes curvy motion with her hands)		
Kevin	Cars have to get drinks from gas stations. Gas makes cars go.		**Machines have human characteristics:** Need to drink as a source of energy.
Ben	There are stoplights so people can walk on roads.		

Figure 4.1. A portion of a COI Observation Record with memos focusing on divergent interpretations of thinking.

　　　　　　　　　　　　　　　From Children's Interests to Children's Thinking

Getting to Know the COI Observation Record Form

The COI Observation Record form (see Appendix 1) is designed to guide teachers who are new to emergent inquiry toward focused observations and to sustain more experienced emergent inquiry teachers with a system to better organize their documentation processes. It consists of three pages for writing observations and inserting observation photos and is modeled after forms typically used for running record observations, with identifier information related to the observers, the date, the participants, and the area where the observation takes place. The memo section of the form diverges from typical running record forms, providing a place for teachers to note their initial thinking (interpretations) of the meaning of children's play. Whether on the spot with a camera, or when using video, the COI Observation Record form will prompt you to document in a way that links the objective details of observed behavior with your initial thinking about children's developing theories and knowledge. This section introduces you to the details of the form.

Identifier Information at the Top of the COI Observation Record Form

Tag

The tag is an organizing, search, and retrieval tool to help you locate documents at any point when you want to revisit them for future planning. It is where you will note the Big Idea or thread of inquiry that the observation links to. In the example in Figure 4.2, the Big Idea is exploring with incinerators and recycling. The Big Idea for the COI Observation Record focusing on the road play in Figure 4.1 was noted by the teacher as early road play in the block center. Examples of tags from the road play as it evolved included additional identification related to specific threads of inquiry being explored:

- Road play in block center: developing community

- Road play in art and literacy: drawing and mapping roads and telling stories about the functions of roads

- Road play in block center: exploring the structure and purposes of bridges

Cycle of Inquiry
Observation Record

OR

Tag: Exploring with Incinerators and Recycling
Interpreters: Christina Raffoul and Freda Shatara

Date:

AREA: Inquiry project area
PARTICIPANTS: Muse, Ryan A., Hassan, JD, Matthew, Tatiana, Renato, Fatme
SETUP: Video is shared with each small project group (on classroom laptop in inquiry project area of classroom)

By working with documentation of children's **actions** and **words** we focus our discussions on evidence and de-privatize our discussions about children's thinking. (Reggio Study Group)

NAMES:	DESCRIPTION:	MEMOS:
Distinguish teachers' names from children's.	**ACTIONS**—(In parentheses) **WORDS**—Not in parentheses	Raise your questions about the meanings of children's actions and words. Why did they do / say this? What do they know?

Figure 4.2. Top section of COI Observation Record form where identifier information is recorded.

Date of observation

Note the date to keep track of the progress of children's developing inquiry.

Observers

Note the specific observer. Coteachers may each have their own styles of recording and interpreting play. These diverse views will influence planning, and it is helpful to be aware of the ways each individual's interpretations influence the progress of the curriculum. You can plan so that you or your coteacher closely observes and documents the inquiry project while the other oversees the activity in the remaining learning centers.

Area

Note the section of the room, building, or grounds where the observation takes place. Knowledge of the area may impact ideas for future planning due to awareness of the affordances—resources with a clear suggestion for use—or drawbacks of the particular space with regard to the children's focus.

Participants

Name all children who are participating to determine the role and impact of each child on the developing inquiry.

Setup

Describe in detail the way the materials are organized at the start of your observation. This section is important because, as you learned in Chapter 1, the environment and materials have a strong influence on the many directions of children's play and guide you to make sense of the play when rereading the observation record. The setup at the start of the example in Figure 4.3 states, "Video is shared with each small project group (on laptop in inquiry project area of classroom)."

Written Observation Data

Left Column: Names

Record the names of each child or adult following the sequence of their play and interactions. When necessary, times can be noted in this column as well. Generally, time codes are not required unless a time sampling is called for, or if you are recording from a video where you would want to note the specific time in order to revisit the video.

- When coding from a video, record the start and end times of the frames being transcribed (e.g., 00.03.21 to 00.10.12). Rather than transcribe the entire video footage, record in writing the sections of video that are significant to your intentions for interpreting play to build curricular plans.

- Distinguishing teachers from children makes it easier to revisit the observation data and visibly see the relationship between children's and teachers' thinking. Color coding is an easy way to make these distinctions. Teachers who are not typing their records often use highlighter markers to color-code their records. (In the observation record in Figures 4.3–4.11, the teacher's name is shown in bold type. In Figure 4.4, there are no names in bold type, which shows that the observing teacher has not verbally entered this conversation.)

Center Column: Description (Actions and Words)

Record both the actions and words of the participants. Distinguishing between actions and words makes it easier to revisit the observation data and visibly see the relationship between the actions and words when interpreting the meaning of the play from the perspective of the child or the adult being observed. So many details of children's thinking are represented by their actions. Often when children are deeply engaged they speak less, as their actions occupy their focus. The actions related to thinking are particularly clear when observing nonverbal infants and toddlers.

Capture sufficient details so that someone not present at the observation can develop a good understanding of the meaning of the play from your observation record. At this phase in the inquiry process, you are seeking information from children. Seek what children have to say in conversations and through their actions. Your prompts may be open ended without an intended outcome other than learning about the children's perspectives on the topic. If you find that children are not responsive to a topic for which you have planned opportunity for conversation, be sure that your interactions are open ended and allow time for children to respond authentically. In addition, take more time to observe children's constructive play experiences to discover and learn more about their thinking.

Visual Documentation Records: Photos or Video Frames as Photos

Photographs that accompany on-the-spot written observation records remind teachers of the level of engagement of the play, although by themselves photographs are not sufficient for planning emergent curriculum. When teachers refer to photographs alone, they recall fewer details. While photos can trigger memories, a lot of important information is forgotten without on-the-spot written records or video.

Video records allow teachers to revisit children's play several times to notice more details than can be recorded in on-the-spot written records. The best part of using a video is being able to listen more carefully to the children as you record because you are not focusing on writing.

Photos and frames of video can be easily inserted into the COI Observation Record form at the end of the written record, or you can include them within the context of the related written records and memos, like those in the example from teachers Christina and Freda later in this chapter. Practice taking photos at the children's level to capture their perspective of their actions, the stages of their thinking processes, and their techniques or strategies with materials.

Right Column: Memos

As stated earlier, the memos section is where you document your initial thinking and interpretations. Include your questions about the meaning of children's actions and words, your thinking about the reasoning behind children's actions and words, and your thoughts on what the children know. If you are inclined, include your own drawings of children's constructions or processes as a way of reflecting on what you observe.

- Aim to record your memos immediately following the play you observe or as close to the play session as possible. Remaining open to divergent ideas that come to mind at this time is valuable for later stages of planning.

- Revisit these memos several times to allow for revision and refinement. Revisiting helps teachers to dig deeper and to view the data in many ways from multiple perspectives.

> For example, the idea that machines need drinks for energy was a new idea that emerged during a later review of the observation focusing on road play in the block area (see Fig. 4.1).

■ Collaborative meetings with coteachers to share and develop diverse interpretations of the observation data help teachers become aware of interpretations or data they may not have considered previously, and this process expands teachers' divergent thinking capacity.

> The thinking about vehicles and roads in Figure 4.1 represented a wide range of interpretations that led to ideas for extensions. These in-depth interpretations were developed in a meeting among two teachers following the observation.

Teachers revisit the observation data in their COI Observation Record forms to develop diverse interpretations.

Using the COI Observation Record Form

Learning from the Incinerator Project

To guide you through the practical use of the COI Observation Record form, this section includes an example completed by two preservice teachers, Christina and Freda, working together as a team. This example represents their collaborative documentation of children's developing understanding of garbage trucks and incinerators. The example follows the sequence of three cycles of the children's emergent inquiry. A cycle refers to each time teachers go through the process of using all of the COI forms. In the documentation of Christina and Freda in Figures 4.3–4.11, you will see that each cycle is represented by a different color of type: black for cycle 1, red for cycle 2, and blue for cycle 3.

Teachers typically observe and document related inquiry experiences many times prior to planning further with the remaining COI forms that are introduced throughout this book (Interpreting Thinking, Curriculum Action Plan, Inquiry Provocation Plan, and Reflective Evaluation). To learn about these processes in the next several chapters, you will follow the ways that Christina and Freda make use of each COI form for the incinerator project.

It is important to note that the three cycles in this example are just the early phases of a long-term project that Christina and Freda guided over three months. As student teachers, they worked within the context of a semester, but practicing classroom teachers often guide long-term emergent inquiry projects through almost an entire school year.

Tag: Exploring with Incinerators and Recycling
Interpreters: Christina Raffoul and Freda Shatara

Date:

AREA: Inquiry project area
PARTICIPANTS: muse, Ryan A., Hassan, JD, Matthew, Tatiana, Renato, Fatme
SETUP: Video is shared with each small project group (on classroom laptop in inquiry project area of classroom)

By working with documentation of children's **actions** and **words** we focus our discussions on evidence and de-privatize our discussions about children's thinking. (Reggio Study Group)

NAMES: Distinguish teachers' names from children's.	DESCRIPTION: ACTIONS—(In parentheses) WORDS—Not in parentheses	MEMOS: Raise your questions about the meanings of children's actions and words. Why did they do / say this? What do they know?
	1/5	
muse	This is the slide for the incinerator.	What part is he referring to as the slide?
Ryan A.	That's where they burn the garbage. (Placing Jenga blocks around the building.) It's sirens. It's to warn the people to get the garbage off of them if they need it.	
	1/8 (Group time video on garbage/incinerators) Setup: Inquiry Project area with video on laptop	
mrs. Holman	Where do garbage trucks go?	
Hassan	It goes to garbage station.	
JD	Everybody's houses.	
muse	It's a garbage dump. I think they call it some kind of land something. Grabbers. They pick up garbage. The hard part is they have to use the controllers.	Research landfills and how the grabbers work. Look at controllers.
mrs. Holman	What does recycle mean? (Paused video.)	
Hassan	When something is old, they make it something new.	Hassan understands the concept of recycling.
matthew	You need to put it in recycle to recycle.	Recycling bins are familiar.
muse	You take something that's old and used and make it in something new again.	muse understands recycling.
Tatiana	We put it in a recycle can. We put it outside.	The children are familiar with recycling and some things they are able to recycle. Including recycling in our inquiry will enhance their understandings.
mrs. Holman	What do you recycle at home?	
muse	Paper.	
Hassan	I recycle a bottle of milk.	
MJ	Leaves.	Compost?
mrs. Holman	What did you learn about the incinerator? (After video.)	
Hassan	All the garbage goes in the fire.	

Figure 4.3. First page of cycle 1 documented by Christina and Freda.

Renato	When the crane picked it up.	
matthew	Put the garbage in the big pile of garbage. It catches on fire and then we can turn our lights on and off.	Electricity.
muse	I learned that it turns into steam.	What is steam? Does he understand how steam forms?

1/8 (PM Investigations: Building with Recycled materials)
Setup: Inquiry Project area. Recycled trash in a bag is opened and shared with group to begin conversation

muse	We're going to make an incinerator. I want to make a grabber.	
Renato	(Pointing to bottles) These move to the fire. (Pointing to plastic container) This can be the grabber. This is what it looks like. (He put it through the conveyor belt.)	
muse	(Put garbage in the grabber, pretending to pick it up.) Okay, it's on the hopper on the conveyor belt. Here is a pile of ash after it goes in the fire. (He and Ian put garbage all over the conveyor belt.) Now all of this is turning into ash! There's a lot of garbage turning into ash.	muse is able to recall the journey garbage takes through the incinerator. How can we help him understand the more minute details?
matthew	It turns into light!	Investigating electricity.
All 3 Boys	(They put the empty paper towel rolls under the plastic bags to act as the conveyor belt.)	How can we create a real conveyor belt?
Renato	(Took a paper towel roll, hooked it on the pop bottle, and created a crane.)	How can we create a crane?
		The children are able to explain their drawings well. We would like them to add more details and eventually use plans to create a model of the incinerator.

Figure 4.4. Second page of cycle 1 documented by Christina and Freda.

1/12 (Incinerator Drawings/ Buildings)
Setup: Art center with paper, pencils, and blocks
for construction of incinerator or conveyor belt

Ryan A.	(Drawing) This is a garbage truck. It takes it to the incinerator.	
muse	(Explaining his drawing) Garbage truck. Landfill. Then, the grabber, then the fire claw. Then, to the hopper.	

1/13 (Building an Incinerator)
Setup: Inquiry project area. Recycled
trash in a bag is opened and shared
with group to begin conversation

	(All of the children worked together to create a conveyor belt for the trash.)	Collaboration is present.
muse	I want to make a claw, so I can pick up the garbage!	
Ms. Raffoul	How does the conveyor belt work?	How can we investigate this concept further?
Ryan A.	You have to press a button.	
	(made an ash truck and pretended the trash turned into ash and then electricity)	

1/15 (Incinerator Drawings/Building)
Setup: Art center with paper, pencils, and blocks
for construction of incinerator or conveyor belt

Hassan	The dump truck puts garbage and the claw gets them. Then, the claw goes up and puts them in the hopper. The garbage goes down. The big thing pushes it into the fire. It turns into ashes, then smoke. It makes electricity and the light we can turn on and off.	Hassan has a good understanding of the sequential process.
Tatiana	(Drew people working in the building)	
muse	Bricks are sturdier and sticks fall down.	How can we build strong and sturdy?

Figure 4.5. Third page of cycle 1 documented by Christina and Freda.

Renato	I made a claw. It grabs all the trash from the truck.	
Ryan A.	I'm making a baby incinerator.	mini incinerator models.
Fatme	I want to make mine really tall. The garbage goes into the fire here.	

1/27 Revisit of Incinerator Video/K-W-L Chart (Small group investigation)

Setup: Art center with paper, pencils, and blocks for construction of incinerator or conveyor belt

Ms. Raffoul	What do you already know about incinerators?	
Ryan A.	The garbage truck comes to the house and takes it to the incinerator and then burns the trash.	
muse	I know that the grabber goes down and picks up the floam and puts it in the feed hopper.	
Ian	I know that the claw goes down and picks it up and drops it.	
J.D.	The claw drops off the garbage. The conveyor belt burns the trash.	
mitchell	The incinerator picks up the garbage and turns it into dust.	
Tatiana	I remember the grabber that swings, and it picks up the recycled bottles. The grabber goes up and down and up and down.	Next step? How does the grabber work?
Renato	I know the claw goes down and picks up the garbage.	
matthew	The grabber picks up the garbage and puts it right in the fire.	misconception. Step is skipped.
Daniel	The garbage goes in the fire.	
Ms. Raffoul	What questions do you have before we watch the video? What are you wondering about?	
muse	I am wondering about how the trash turns into ash.	
J.D.	How does the claw move?	

Figure 4.6. Fourth page of cycle 1 and beginning of cycle 2 documented by Christina and Freda.

Ian	I don't know how the claw moves.	
Tatiana	I am wondering about how the claw works.	
Renato	I am wondering about the claw and how it picks up garbage.	*Investigate funnels and how the feed hopper works.
J.D.	*While watching the video: There are a lot of different ones (watching part about trash cans). They are all different shapes. What is that? (Claw that picks up the metal in ash) It looks like a box. (Recycled materials all together) Those are clocks. (Temperature gauges) 	
Ms. Raffoul	What did you learn after watching the video?	
muse	I learned how they get the trash into ash. They put it in the fire (pushing motion). The grabber is my favorite part.	
Ryan A.	When it burns garbage.	
J.D.	The crane picks up the garbage, and then takes it to the feed hopper. My favorite part is the crane.	
Ian	I learned how the crane moves. The crane is my favorite part.	
Tatiana	I learned that the grabber goes up and down and puts the trash in the feed hopper. Then it goes in the tunnel, and then I learned that the box fills the garbage.	How does the grabber actually move up and down?
matthew	It goes into the garbage truck factory. The incinerator cleans up, and it goes in the foo-hopper.	
Daniel	The garbage goes in the fire, and it turns into ash.	
Ms. Raffoul	What do you want to learn more about?	
Tatiana	Feed hopper.	
matthew	The incinerator cleans up. Claw goes up and goes in foo-hopper.	
Renato	The garbage truck dumping it.	

Figure 4.7 Second page of cycle 2 documented by Christina and Freda.

Daniel	The trucks.	
	1/29 Revisit of Incinerator Video/K-W-L Chart (Second group) *All other documentation is on K-W-L chart. Setup: Inquiry project area with group, photos, and chart	
Ms. Shatara	What do you already know about incinerators?	
James	They grab it, and then they drop it. When there is a big stack of garbage, it will fall down. A guy gets in it and moves it.	
Hassan	The grabber puts the garbage in the hopper. It goes down and something pushed it in the fire, and it turns into ash.	
Ms. Shatara	Where have you seen a funnel before? Maybe sand?	
Hassan	Yeah, I have!	
Ms. Shatara	Why do you think air is added? (While watching the part about the combustion chamber)	Trying to make a connection with the feed hopper and how they have used funnels.
James	Air makes fire go.	
Ali	When the air pushes it in, it gets big.	Videos on starting a fire? Could we actually do this at school?
Ms. Shatara	What is electricity?	
Ryan R.	It makes things work.	
Renato	It makes things turn on and off.	Yes!
Ms. Shatara	Where do you see it?	
Fatme	The lights! The light table!	
Hassan	The lamp.	
Ms. Shatara	How does the lamp light up?	
Hassan	The white wire connects it.	Hassan has prior knowledge on wires and electric circuits.
Ms. Shatara	What do you want to know or still wonder about?	
Hassan	The hopper.	
James	The grabber.	
Fatme	About how it [the grabber] works inside the truck.	
Ali	The garbage truck. How do they fix it when it breaks?	
Milani	The parts. How they work.	
Matthew	How long? (Talking about the whole process) Why do the lights burn out?	*Add to COI Questions form Why do the lights burn out?

Figure 4.8. Third page of cycle 2 documented by Christina and Freda.

From Children's Interests to Children's Thinking

	2/3 Exploring Handheld Claws (1st group of children) Setup: Inquiry project area with handheld claws and trash	
muse	I saw it in the garbage video.	
J.D	This is the claw's mouth. (Pointed to the claw)	
Hassan	It puts it in the pusher. The hopper.	
muse	It's too fat! (Picked up tube)	
Hassan	When you push down, it opens and closes.	
J.D	The smaller claw opens easier.	
muse	I squeeze it together.	
muse & Hassan	(Passed bottles with grabbers)	Hassan notices the cause/effect we were hoping the children would want to further explore.

J.D	(Piling materials) That's the garbage.	
Hassan	It's too fat. (Pushes together harder)	
Ryan A.	I'm the big claw.	
muse	Move it to the feed hopper. You just have to pull it back. It controls it, and you can grab stuff. Let's move all the garbage right here.	What does he mean by control?
Ian	We're making a pile.	
Fatme	The claws are picking up the garbage.	
James	Take it to the roaster. (Putting things on, instead of grabbing)	Is the roaster the combustion chamber?

Figure 4.9. First page of cycle 3 documented by Christina and Freda.

Ian	I got two things at once.
Ian & Renato	When you put it up, it closes.
Fatme	Open, close, open, close. The claw is picking up (Transferring).
Ian	Now it turns to ash.
Renato	Stay away from this. It's the feed hopper. It's dangerous. There is fire at the bottom.
Teacher	How is it like the big claw?
muse	It can grab stuff.
Renato	It looks bigger and better. It can pick up more things. These are just pretend claws.
Fatme	These claws are small. You can pinch.
Renato	The claws put them in the feed hopper.
matthew	(Holding a small crate with grabber and transferring trash in it)
Teacher	How does it work?
matthew	Push here. It closes.
Teacher	But it's so far away. How can it close it?
matthew	This metal thing. It goes through it. Then, it closes.
Renato	(Swinging it and moving trash) Beep, beep! FedEx!
J.D	(Pulled lever up and down) It helps the claw open and close. (Pointing to the claw) This is the claw's mouth, and he's eating everything.
	2/3 Revisiting after lesson (Group time) Setup: Inquiry project area with group and chart
ms. m.	What did you think? Do?
Ryan A	I opened it and couldn't get the fat tube because it's too fat.
muse	I discovered that if I put the claw in Ryan's pocket, I can grab it.

Thinking ahead to the next step in the process.

The children are able to make connections with these claws and the big claw.

Pinch vs grabbing with the bigger claw of the incinerator?

matthew knows that it cannot close on its own, something needs to connect it.

Figure 4.10. Second page of cycle 3 documented by Christina and Freda.

Hassan	We can grab tubes from each other's claws.	
Muse	My grabber was stronger than the other. I could take it when it's closed.	
James	I pushed the button to make it go. The thing that pushes it into the fire.	
Fatme	Claws can open and close. Open, grab up garbage, close it.	
	2/5 Exploring Handheld Claws (2nd group of children) Setup: Inquiry project area with handheld claws and trash	
Tatiana Maia	I'm pushing the black part and it opens (using two hands). (Pressing down on the lever)	
Ms. S.	(Opening the claw up to show how the black part moves) How does it move?	
Tatiana	The black part moves up and down! They're [tubes] large. They're going in the feed hopper.	Great problem solving!
Maia	(Grabbed the large tubes by turning the claw and picking them up from the inside, instead of around the tube)	Investigate misconceptions in the next lesson. What is actually inside of the grabber?
Ryan R.	You have to grab slowly. You have to do it sideways.	
Renato	It goes back and forth and opens and shuts. When you pull it back, it closes. When you don't pull it back, it opens.	
Ms. S.	What do you think is inside the claw?	
Ryan R.	Wood.	
Renato	Maybe if we open it, we'll find out!	
Howie	Gears.	
Ian	Something long.	
Ryan R.	(Picks garbage up with the claw and puts it over his head in a swinging motion)	Ryan remembers the motion of the claw from the incinerator.
Ms. S.	How is the big claw different than these claws?	
Howie	The big claw has more things [pinchers].	
Renato	The little claw picks up less.	
Hassan	It's really big.	
Ms. S.	How do the grabbers move in the incinerator?	
Hassan	The people who work it. It goes down and picks up garbage. They push a button. They use handles. (moved his hands in a handle motion)	Explore the controllers and handles of the incinerator.
Ian	(Held up his grabber, made it go straight down and picked up garbage. He then swung it to the side and let go of the garbage.) The real incinerator only has one claw.	Ian is mimicking the motion the claw makes in the incinerator.
Muse	The claw is bigger, so it can pick up more stuff.	

Figure 4.11. Third page of cycle 3 documented by Christina and Freda.

COI Checklists

The COI system has checklists for you to identify and assess your skill development with the practices of each phase of the COI process. Checklists support the development of meta-reflective teachers who are able to articulate their practices, give evidence to support what they are doing, and integrate knowledge from one interpretation to another. The checklist for each COI form can be used by teachers, directors, teaching teams, and researchers as targets to aim for when learning to plan and implement emergent inquiry curriculum. Use the COI Observation Record Checklist (see Appendix 1) to decide if you have collected enough information to interpret play and develop next steps in an emergent inquiry process.

Observation Checklist Criteria to Guide Successful Use of the COI Observation Record Form

This section provides a review of the COI Observation Record forms Christina and Freda completed in relation to criteria from the COI Observation Record Checklist.

Amount and Nature of the Data

Christina and Freda relied on the following criteria to provide many examples of detailed play episodes, each with in-depth meaning, on their observation records.

Did you capture sufficient detail to interpret the episode?

In this example, the preservice teachers took advantage of documenting several classroom sessions centered on the children's exploration of garbage disposal and recycling. The documentation data for each of three cycles were collected over many days of exploration and observation. You can see how these teachers entered the date into the form each time they documented. This allowed them to observe for several days, as needed, to follow the evolution of a process and to collect a substantial amount of appropriate data prior to moving on to the next phase in the COI, the interpretation phase, which requires deeper reflection and interpretation.

These preservice teachers initiated their documentation process when they noticed the topic emerge spontaneously during play. Children were pretending to pick up trash and put it into a place where garbage is burned, which they referred to as an incinerator. To assess children's knowledge and interest, Christina and Freda brought in a video on garbage incineration to expand the conversation. They continued to document during this focused classroom meeting with the entire class, which brought the thinking of a small group investigation to the whole class.

Two final sources for the observation data in this example were (1) the investigation session where children were designing and building an incinerator, and (2) the small core group opportunity for revisiting, provided by teachers for the children to deepen their understanding about the functions of the various components of a garbage truck and incinerator. There was great potential for teachers to develop their understanding of children's purposes when they focused on and captured observation data from a variety of play experiences that were conceptually linked. Christina and Freda recognized that the children were demonstrating a growing ability for using their imagination to visualize solutions (using claws to pick up garbage) and new concepts (the transformation of fire into energy like light), one of the many science concepts identified in this project that are linked to early learning standards for this age group. In Chapter 8 you will see how Christina and Freda identified many of the state early learning standards that children addressed through these experiences.

Did you document connected events to describe a meaningful play episode?

In this example, the connected events were intentionally planned by the preservice teachers. In the initial observation, teachers were inspired by children's enactment of garbage and incinerators. The second observation provided opportunity to use a video clip to focus conversations on children's understanding of the incinerators and to generate new ideas from the children. The investigation and revisiting sessions with the children gave them a chance to apply their ideas to inventive processes and to synthesize throughout the project. These applications are linked to early learning cognitive development and science standards. Christina and Freda recorded the children's play and discussion until they obtained enough information to describe and interpret the children's thought processes.

Did you follow the connected events even if they moved from place to place?

This play moved from the block area to the inquiry project area, then on to the writing center where the drawing processes occurred, and back to the inquiry project area. Christina and Freda captured continuous play that incorporated a wide range of ideas and explorations over several days. Their sequence of documenting on the COI Observation Record form indicates that they pursued observations related to garbage and incineration in many areas of the classroom.

Did you include photographs or video clips?

Visual documentation helps to elaborate on the details of the observed play.

- From the level of the child: At least one photo in Christina and Freda's example was captured in each exploration to support the COI Observation Record. All photos focused on the children's actions and showed that the teachers were thinking from the children's perspective. The photos demonstrated children's depth of engagement.

- Of the steps in the child's thinking process: Christina and Freda didn't take many photos that showed the children's thinking process in steps, like photos showing the process of drawing an incinerator, at the start and throughout. However, they included photos of the actions of many children that showed each child's engagement and strategy, like lining up plastic bags to represent a long and linear conveyor belt or using claws to pick up and transport trash.

- Of the child's strategies/techniques with materials: The photos in this example showed that the children were manipulating objects with their hands or tools. These moments revealed their strategies. When the children drew the incinerator, the teacher zoomed in with the camera lens to capture the details of their drawings.

- Of the emotion of the child (if this is significant to the documentation focus): Many photos in the example demonstrated the children's intense focus on their work.

Accuracy and Ease of Use of the Data

The ideas in this section will help you easily read your observation data when you revisit for planning.

Did you distinguish dialogue from action?

Christina and Freda used parentheses to describe complex actions and distinguish actions from dialogue. This made it easy for them to scan their COI Observation Record to see the ways actions and dialogue influenced the children's thinking.

Did you distinguish teachers from children?

In the example, the use of the teachers' formal names served as an identifier for the teachers, Mrs. Holman and Ms. Raffoul. In classrooms where teachers are referred to by their first name, a color code, such as blue for teacher names, can be used to distinguish children from teachers.

Did you invent methods for recording complex behavior or products?

A strategy these teachers used to record complex interactions among children was to record the play title and date of each play episode. As they recorded their observations on different days on the same COI Observation Record form, Christina and Freda labeled the date and the title of each day of play in a bold font within parentheses. They also included information about the setup of each play experience.

Did you produce a clear, descriptive transcript of important processes and products you observed?

Christina and Freda transcribed the entire episode to follow the sequence of play and the resulting discussion as it unfolded, using several clear descriptions of the processes and outcomes of the children's exploration. Many descriptions focused on detailed nonverbal actions and verbal expressions and the cause-and-effect relationships of the play.

Focus on Children's Thinking and on Your Thinking

The memos are where you first record your spontaneous ideas about the observations and your questions and speculations about what you notice.

Did you separate your speculations and thinking from your observations?

There are no interpretive statements in the body of the running record data in the example. Christina and Freda clearly separated their speculations by recording them in the memos column.

Did you relate children's actions to their possible goals or theories?

There are several examples of the teachers' thinking about children's goals and theories. In the first cycle on January 5 (Fig. 4.3), the teachers acknowledged the children's idea about landfills and the need to research this topic. In their second observation, on January 8, they recognized the children's theories about the process of garbage moving through an incinerator. In the third observation, also on January 8, they further recognized the children's desire to understand the concepts involved from garbage pickup through to incineration.

Did you think about links to previous play episodes in your memos?

Christina and Freda intentionally focused on children's ideas when they observed. This is evident through their facilitation and documentation of garbage recycling, video viewing, drawing the incinerator, and building with recycled materials. These play episodes were intentionally linked for several days around related content.

Did you think about your questions as ideas for plans to extend children's thinking?

As Christina and Freda reviewed their observation records, their questions related to content that might be explored further with children. Ideas related to expanding children's current knowledge and thinking.

For Further Reflection and Inquiry

This chapter has introduced you to the significance of carefully documenting the details of intentional observations as the basis for developing long-term emergent inquiry curriculum. We recommend that you take the time to practice working with the observation record to develop your skills before continuing on to the next chapter, which outlines the next step in the COI planning processes. Becoming clear on what to observe and the details you capture in writing, photo, video, or audio will prepare you for digging deeper into the process of interpreting the meaning of children's play.

For deeper reflection on observing with intention in your classroom, try these suggestions:

1. List the information about observing that is new to you and discuss with your coteacher, teaching team, or director.

2. List the information about documenting observations that is new to you and discuss with your coteacher, director, or teaching team.

3. Look through the sorts of observations you have been using in your program to compare how they are similar to and different from the COI Observation Record form. Then discuss with your coteacher, teaching team, or director how the information in this chapter will impact your observation practice.

4. Discuss the ways you will benefit from documenting initial thinking (interpretations) with your coteacher, teaching team, or director.

5. Discuss the ways you currently use photo documentation and new ways you will work with photo or video in your future practice with your coteacher, teaching team, or director.

CHAPTER 5
Interpreting Children's Thinking

Every aspect of the COI system involves your thoughts on how children's thinking is guiding the curriculum. Your interpretations connect your description of children's play to your ideas of what children have in mind. Through these descriptions you create theories about what the children are thinking (Carter 2018; Wien & Halls 2018). These descriptions generally surface in casual conversations among teachers following their observations, when they excitedly share what they noticed. This chapter introduces the COI Interpreting Thinking form, which asks you to acknowledge the significance of this reflective thinking and these shared conversations by documenting them in the form of a descriptive narrative focusing on what you see as significant in your observation records. Writing a narrative helps you to reflect on and better understand children's thinking and to plan based on children's perspectives (Carter 2018; Curtis 2017). As you practice this writing process, you will likely generate more ideas about observation data than you would through undocumented conversation.

see shadows when the room is very, very dark. She bases her drawing on her knowledge of two things: that in the very dark room she could not see her shadow and that her shadow is attached to her when the light is on. The things children do suggest that they believe the world acts in a particular way—which it might in some circumstances but not in others. If you interpret children's actions as strategies, you can use them as indications of what children may be thinking. Although you are speculating, if you stay open minded you can form a number of theories and questions about the children's thinking that you can explore with them (Forman & Hall 2005; Silveira & Curtis 2018). Your interpretations of the many details within children's thinking is a bit like brainstorming, which is a divergent thinking process. These ideas can guide you to intervene to challenge children's theories.

Teacher Interpretation
Teacher Thinking About Children's Thinking

The most fruitful behaviors to identify in your observation records for extending children's thinking are those that suggest some strategy the child is using to achieve a goal based on her existing knowledge. These strategies give meaning to the child's actions. For example, Lizzy is drawing a shadow in what she describes as her tummy. As she draws, she tells her teacher and her friends, who are also drawing, that the lights have been turned off and the shadow went inside her. Her goal is to think about why she doesn't

Teachers collaborate to revisit and interpret the observation data in their COI Observation Record forms.

A planning goal is to design ways you can intervene with materials, statements, or questions so that children may act in ways that challenge their own thinking. This self-challenging process is at the heart of constructive play (DeVries et al. 2002; Duckworth 2006; Fosnot 2005; Jones 2012). The goal is for materials, statements, or questions to be subtle enough that children feel as if they are the authority, challenging themselves as they explore and engage in peer conversations. When you focus on children's developing theories, consider what you might do to give them opportunities to test or extend their thinking (Wien & Halls 2018). Through experimentation children gain new knowledge. For example, as a first-step provocation to extend Lizzy's thinking about shadows, her teachers set up a center with a stationary light that is safe for children to turn off and on, a large box prepared with a window cut out, and three pieces of materials of different thickness to cover the window. Children could manipulate light inside and outside the box to explore the position of shadows.

Interpreting Children's Goals and Related Strategies

Children's actions and words mean something to you because they give you information about children's development, personalities, emotional needs, interests, and knowledge and theories of the world. To develop emergent inquiry curriculum, you will focus on ways to better understand and extend children's developing knowledge and theories of the world. Develop the habit of speculating on the ways children are *thinking*: "the children are acting this way because they have a goal or a strategy for achieving that goal" (Carter 2018; Forman & Hall 2005; Wien & Halls 2018).

A Focus on Thinking Leads to Conceptual Versus Thematic Curricular Design

To understand the difference between planning conceptually and planning thematically, consider a classroom in which several children are actively playing with dinosaur characters they find in the block area. A teacher who is not paying close attention to the thinking behind the children's use of the dinosaurs might immediately think about dinosaurs as the "what" of the behavior. Seeing this as an interest, she introduces activities for building a dinosaur habitat. In contrast, a teacher who tries to understand the children's behavior takes note of the details, like the ways the children are using words, growls, and actions to possibly represent the "bigness" of dinosaurs. She hypothesizes that bigness is an idea the children have in mind. Unsure, she invites the children to look through several historical and informational books about dinosaurs, including encyclopedias.

The children's dialogue and actions again seem to reveal that they are more than likely intrigued by the bigness of these creatures. They use blocks to construct what they speak of as tall and strong dinosaurs. They pause on a picture of a dinosaur claw that leads them into a rich discussion about size, wondering how big the dinosaur's claw would be in comparison to their fingernails. Thus, bigness and scale become the focus of this teacher's plans to help the children extend and investigate their thinking and theories about these concepts. The difference between the two teachers is a themed focus versus a conceptual focus that follows and builds on the children's theories.

Power might also be of interest with these large creatures, as it might be when children pretend to be superheroes. In these situations, teachers can guide children to think about their ideas about power and authority, their role in the world in relation to powerful adults and such, rather than create blanket rules to ban superhero or power play. For example, a preschool teacher and director who investigated "bad guys" with 4-year-old children found that the rich conversations in their long-term process of exploring ideas about bad guys and good guys helped children to express feelings that surfaced at night and just before sleep. This reduced the representation of bad-guy play in the classroom.

Following her first experiences with the COI Interpreting Thinking form, Christine, a director in a Reggio-inspired preschool in Virginia, reflected on the need to interpret closely in order to avoid a themed curriculum and to design plans that truly align with the children's purposes:

> *Interpreting thinking* is the part in the cycle that I think most teachers miss. What is behind the child's actions? What are they thinking? What are they questioning or trying to figure out? This is really the key pivot in the cycle and critical to development of curriculum. It's probably the most important form to take the time and reflect on. Although time consuming, this part of the process in the development of curriculum is really the whole point, the crux of the matter. . . . I believe many teachers might capture the essence of children's exploration and derive a "themed" curriculum without truly reflecting on interpreting thinking.

Writing about what they think the children are thinking in a narrative description is a very new experience for many teachers. It is a stretch to look at documentation of the children's actions and circumstances and determine what the children's thought processes may be. As noted previously, teachers have been trained to be objective, having been told that the subjective nature of interpretation is taboo. Tina, a graduate student studying early childhood, expressed the way she feels challenged when asked to interpret children's thinking:

> Teachers have been trained to take notes without thinking. We are told to write what we see, be objective, don't write what we think. We are, in a sense, being trained to *not* think about why. I think it is going to really take some time to retrain teachers to think about what they are writing and get them to try to figure out about children's thinking.

Teachers need to think of the "why" more than "what". . . . Think about children's work in terms of "why they are doing what they are doing" as opposed to "what are they doing." I think this is the biggest challenge in regard to observation and documentation.

Janet, a teacher, also noted the importance of focusing on the why of a child's behavior:

> I observed a boy who built a structure out of bricks and rolled a marble down the ramp and his structure did not fall. I noticed that he continued to build on the structure and he still got the same results. Then I realized that his purpose was not to knock down the structure but to make a structure that would not fall when he rolled the marble. I would have not thought of that if I hadn't observed and reflected on his thinking.

The COI Interpreting Thinking Form
What to Document

When you have the impulse to share your thoughts about the play you've just observed and documented, or when you have the opportunity to review your observation records, you will want to capture your thinking in the COI Interpreting Thinking form (see Appendix 2). The meaningful events of the play will come to mind in the act of describing a play episode as a narrative. Write quickly, organizing the narrative to read like a good story that (1) has a point, (2) gives brief background description, and (3) focuses on events that move the story along. To ensure that your descriptions are useful for planning a curriculum, base them on observation details that suggest children are using specific strategies. You cannot always tell what the strategies are, but you can form good guesses or imagine provocations that will help you to further explore the children's thinking beyond the what to the why. Use lots of descriptive language so you can identify actions that seem significant, but also capture your speculations about children's thinking in your narration to get to the heart of children's theories:

- I think they did this because of that.

- Are they thinking this or that when they do this or that?

- Why do they think their actions are reasonable?

- What do I think are their goals?

- What do I think they want to see happen?

Interpret a child's actions as strategies when you think he is using some knowledge or theory to achieve a goal (Forman & Hall 2005). If you interpret actions as indications of a child's interests only, these may suggest where the child is developmentally, or a particular interest, an emotional or social need, or a personality trait. It is fine to note these, but these interest indicators typically guide thinking toward themed curriculum around a topic. Topics may hold children's interest for a while but may only accidently challenge children's theories and knowledge about the world (or themselves) and are not likely to probe and extend their thinking.

Strategies for Writing the Narrative

Teachers can capture interpretive thoughts during observations, jotting these down in the memos section of the COI Observation Record form, but understanding the significance of these events usually requires a conversation. These are joyful conversations where teachers learn so much about children's cleverness and wit as well as about their own teaching practices, which energizes them. These collaborative conversations typically take place in the form of teacher meetings, where coteachers or teams of teachers rehash the experiences documented in their observation records.

A recommendation to save time during these conversations is to have one teacher write as another talks about his interpretations. When the writer begins to talk, pass the pencil to another teacher. Capturing the conversation in writing as it progresses means that you won't need to backtrack to record these thoughts and saves precious planning time.

Getting to Know the COI Interpreting Thinking Form

Use the COI Interpreting Thinking form to record the conversations with your coteachers about what you observed and your hypotheses about the children's goals, strategies, and theories. This form has the same identifier information as the COI Observation Record form: a tag for noting the Big Idea or inquiry thread and the observation date. This form asks only for the interpreter's names. There is a top section of a table and a bottom section of a table.

Top Section: Speculate on What the Children Are Doing and Thinking

The top section of the COI Interpreting Thinking form is where you write your narrative, recording your thoughts about what you observed and describing the sequence of events with a story line. You may find that you begin by describing what happened without pausing to think about the reasoning behind children's actions and words. You will want to slow down as you recall the events to tell your story with as much detail as possible, because each bit of detail can represent different strategies or possibilities for extended learning opportunities. To record your thinking about the why and how of the specifics in the children's play, insert language like "I think they did x because they were thinking y" or "action x seems to represent the child's idea y."

The purpose of this form is to begin to think divergently by interpreting the observed play of children from as many perspectives as possible to try to determine what the children might be thinking and what they know. Write your narrative as a series of interpretations. Review the descriptive narrative in Figure 5.1, which represents the many interpretations within an observation of 3- to 5-year-old children exploring worms.

Several Big Ideas for planning next steps that might surface from these interpretations are the ways different animals move, the functions of the body parts of particular animals or humans, and the adaptation of an animal to the environment.

A couple of ideas that emerged in these teachers' particular explorations were the children's thoughts on the relationship of movement to life and lack of movement to death, and the idea of the environment, such as the earth, as a protector from the sun and rain—much in the way that houses serve the same role for the children and their families.

Children exploring a worm with their teacher

Cycle of Inquiry
Interpreting Thinking

IT

Tag:
Interpreters:

Date:

Speculate on what the children are doing and thinking.

In the next two boxes, keep in mind that you're looking for emerging threads of play that have the most potential for advancing play toward children's inquiry. *You are forming a context for interpreting what you saw*.

Write a narrative using as much ***descriptive language*** as possible to tell the reader what you think this play was about. Write freely. Within your description, ***speculate with statements*** like "I think they are doing X because of Y."

The children started play by touching the worms and placing them on the plex-glass table. This was done possibly to gain control of the worm's movements. The children understand that if they change where the worm is then it may affect the movement of their bodies. I think the child understand that since worms do not make noises that they use their bodies to show how they feel. The children have also begun to make hypotheses about the movement of worms because they are able to describe how and why the worms move in different places. The children also are creating cause and effect methods to help back up their hypothesis either stated out loud to a teacher or mentally thought about during engaged manipulation of the worm. Furthermore, the children are beginning to mimic their bodies in comparison to the worm's bodies because they are curious on what it is like to be a worm. Pretend play about being a worm has been evident.

Figure 5.1. Narrative on a COI Interpreting Thinking form representing young children's exploration of worms.

Bottom Section: Thinking from the Child's Perspective

The descriptive process in the first section of the COI Interpreting Thinking form slows down your mind so that you can begin to think from the child's perspective. In this second section you are asked to go a bit further into your ideas about the child's mind by adding statements that you imagine might represent the child's internal thinking or inner speech, such as the following interpretation from the exploration of incinerators (see Fig. 5.3), which had claw parts:

I see the metal part sticking out from the bottom. When I pushed the handle down, it moved. When it moved, the claw closed. I think the metal part makes the claw close.

These are thoughts that Christina and Freda hypothesized. Such invention to try to empathize with the child is not easy but helps teachers come as close to the child's thinking and purposes as possible.

You need to feel what it might be like to be in that child's play, imagining being inside the child's experience (Baker & Davila 2018), and yet speculate as a knowledgeable adult about how that child's mind is working—that is, representing ideas about the play as a responsive observer (Baker & Davila 2018; Silveira & Curtis 2018). When you revisit your observations, maintain a sense that you really don't know just how a child's mind works. As you interpret the thinking of one child, consider the relationship of the child's thinking to the dynamic of the group in which the child is a participant.

Remember that children are not working toward abstract standards. Standards are adult checklists. Children are driven by the workings of their own minds. Take seriously the need for you to develop a robust knowledge of the content in areas children are exploring to better enable provocations that lead them forward in thinking. This may require research on your part.

Children effortlessly weave many ideas through their play episodes that may be tightly or loosely linked together in their minds. What you see as an adult may not be in their minds at all, so through all your planning you need to coach yourself to explore the children's perspectives. Where you may see children making clay shapes, they may actually be testing the properties of materials; they may be enjoying feeling big where you see them as excited about dinosaurs. Seek to coax your adult mind to visit the child's world.

Using the COI Interpreting Thinking Form
Learning from the Incinerator Project

This section provides a review of the COI Interpreting Thinking forms completed by Christina and Freda (see Figs. 5.2 and 5.3) in relation to criteria that comes directly from the COI Interpreting Thinking Checklist (see Appendix 2). The following review builds on their observation records for the incinerator project. As stated previously, we are following three of their COI cycles throughout this book for you to understand the connection of one form to the next in your planning processes. The first cycle, in black font, refers to ten days of observation prior to moving on to this interpretation phase. The second, in red, represents interpretations from eight days of observations, and the third, in blue, represents interpretations from two days of observation. The length of time you will observe prior to moving on to interpreting will vary depending on the number of observation records you have that are related to your inquiry focus.

Documentation related to Christina and Freda's COI Interpreting Thinking form

Tag:

Interpreters: Christina Raffoul and Freda Shatara

Date:

Speculate on what the children are doing and thinking.

In the next two boxes, keep in mind that you're looking for emerging threads of play that have the most potential for advancing play toward children's inquiry. *You are forming a context for interpreting what you saw.*

Write a narrative using as much *descriptive language* as possible to tell the reader what you think this play was about. Write freely. Within your description, *speculate with statements* like "I think they are doing X because of Y."

We think the children are interested in incinerators and how they work. We think they know the basics of how they work because of the video we watched and how detailed some of their responses were. For example, Hassan said, "The dump truck puts garbage and the claw gets them. Then, the claw goes up and puts them in the hopper. The garbage goes down. The big thing pushes it into the fire. It turns into ashes, then smoke. It makes electricity and the light we can turn on and off." The children are also interested in building incinerators. We know this because after we watched the video, we had a material exploration with recycled materials. The children immediately decided to create an incinerator. We think they are the most interested in the conveyor belt and how it works. We think this because this is the main part they were building and discussing how they needed to put the garbage on it and make it move. When asked how they can make it move, Ryan A. said, "Push the button." They put the empty paper towel rolls under the plastic bags and pushed "trash" across it. We think this was acting as their conveyor belt because of the motion of pulling materials across it. The children were also interested in the end product of electricity. After the ash truck took the ash away, Matthew said, "It makes light!"

After going through the K–W–L chart with the children and determining where their interests and focuses are, we think the children are interested in how the grabber/claw works and why it works the way it does. We know this because each time we asked the children what questions they had and what they were interested in learning more about, the majority of their answers revolved around the claw/grabber somehow. For example, Tatiana said, "I am wondering about how the claw works." J.D. also asked, "How does the claw move?" The children are also interested in how the trash turns into ash, and then turns into electricity. We know this because the children asked questions about that part of the process. For example, Muse said, "I am wondering about how the trash turns into ash." On the same idea, Renato also said, "I'm wondering about how the machine makes the garbage into electricity. How does the machine move the trash around in a ball?" These responses tell us that the children are focused on those specific processes and want to know about cause and effect. The second group of children were very interested in the claw, as well. For example, when asked what he already knows about incinerators, Hassan said, "The grabber puts the garbage in the hopper. It goes down and something pushed it in the fire, and it turns into ash." Also, one child also brought up two new ideas, which we hope to eventually expand upon. For example, when Ms. Shatara asked Matthew what he was still wondering about after watching the video, he said, "How long does the whole thing take?" and then "Why do lights burn out?"

We think the children are interested in how the claws move based on the fact that they explored with picking up different sized materials. We also noticed that the children seemed to understand the idea of cause and effect in regard to the claws. For example, when Ms. Shatara asked Matthew how the claw works, he said, "When you push here, it closes." When she asked him how the lever closes the claw when it is so far away from it, Matthew replied, "This metal thing. It goes through it. Then, it closes." This tells us that he was able to make the connection between the cause (what is happening at the top of the claw/grabber with the lever) and the effect (whether the claw opens or closes). The children were able to compare the small grabbers with the large one they observed in the incinerator video. Muse said, "The claw is bigger, so it can pick up more stuff." This shows that he understands that the larger an object is the more volume it has and the more it is able to carry in general. The children were also mimicking the motion of the big claw. Ian held up his grabber, made it go straight down, and picked up garbage. He then swung it to the side and let go of the garbage.

Figure 5.2. Top section of COI Interpreting Thinking form example from Christina and Freda, including cycles 1 to 3.

Look at the above paragraph. Imagine you are the child/children you wrote about. Be those children and write what you are thinking. (We ask you to complete this task to help you dig a bit more deeply into the perspective of the child.)

Hassan—"The dump truck puts garbage and the claw gets them. Then, the claw goes up and puts them in the hopper. The garbage goes down. The big thing pushes it into the fire. It turns into ashes, then smoke. It makes electricity and the light we can turn on and off."
I know from the video that the dump truck puts the garbage in something and the claw gets it next. Then, the claw puts it in the hopper, where the garbage goes down. There is a big thing that puts it into the fire and turns it to ash. Ash turns into smoke and that makes electricity. I drew each part on my paper to show what goes first and last.

Ryan A. — "Push the button."
I know that when I push buttons, things happen. When I push the on button on the TV, it turns on. When I press the button on my toy, it moves.

All of the children were putting the empty paper towel rolls under the plastic bags and pushing "trash" across it. We know the trash goes on the conveyor belt. The conveyor belt moves to take the trash to the new place. We used paper towel rolls because they are round and they roll, making the bags move easier.

Renato—"I'm wondering about how the machine makes the garbage into electricity."
The video says that it turns into electricity, but I don't know how it does it. When I plug things in, they turn on and off. How does garbage do this?

Tatiana—"I am wondering about how the claw works."
I can see it move and pick up the trash, but what makes it move? How does it work?

Matthew—"Why do lights burn out?"
Electricity makes things work. If the lamp is plugged in, then how come they stop working sometimes? What makes them burn out?

Matthew—"This metal thing. It goes through it. Then, it closes."
I see the metal part sticking out from the bottom. When I pushed the handle down, it moved. When it moved, the claw closed. I think the metal part makes the claw close.

Ian — (Held up his grabber, made it go straight down and picked up garbage. He then swung it to the side and let go of the garbage.)
I remember watching the video and seeing how the claw works. It goes straight down and picks up a lot of trash. Then, it swings over to the feed hopper and drops it. It does this over and over again.

Muse — "The claw is bigger, so it can pick up more stuff."
When I play in the sand with my dad, he picks up more sand in his hands than I do. I think this is because he has bigger hands than me. The claw for the incinerator is bigger than these claws, so it can pick up more — like my dad's hands.

Figure 5.3. Bottom section of COI Interpreting Thinking form example from Christina and Freda, including cycles 1 to 3.

Focus on Children's Knowledge and Thinking

Checking the depth of your interpretations about children's thinking supports your reflective practice and planning for next steps.

Did You Describe Significant Events in the Children's Play?

Christina and Freda revisited the Observation Record and video documentation and focused on the curiosity children had about the relationship between garbage and incinerators. The teachers also described their thinking in relation to evidence of the children's evolving representation and engagement in discussion and the creation of a conveyor belt.

Did You Capture Your Thoughts About Why These Events Were Significant?

The teachers referenced the children's words and actions to interpret the meaning of their play in detail. They continued to build hypotheses in relation to the meaning of the children's play with each aspect of the children's processes through the discussion, video, and investigations.

Did You Interpret Events as Indicators of the Thinking of the Children, Not Just Their Interests or Needs?

The narrative describes the children's desire to understand the garbage disposal process in depth, meaning it is not a superficial interest. The teachers' interpretation dug deeper into the developing knowledge and specific thinking about the function of the claws, the role of the conveyor belt, and even the cycle of electrical energy production from garbage through to incineration, which, according to the children, made "light."

Did You Speculate on the Goals Behind the Actions of the Children?

The narrative of the children's conversation illustrated that they wanted to understand how incinerators work. The teachers also recognized the children's goals for making a functional incinerator using materials available to them in their classroom, as children modeled their understanding of how a conveyor belt works by pushing trash across a plastic bag and using a paper towel roll to make it move. There is commentary in Figure 5.2 about children seeking end results, like making electricity, that match what they observed in the video on incinerators.

The teachers used all of this information to develop lesson plans to assist children in learning about these processes.

Did You Speculate on What Knowledge and Theories of the World Made These Actions Strategic or Sensible to Children?

The interpretations in Figure 5.3 focused on the children's theories about the relationship between action (the claw puts the garbage in the hopper) and the effect of the action (the garbage goes down). The words not in bold font represent what children actually said. The words in bold font are those Christina and Freda imagined the children might have been saying internally, using inner speech to represent their theories. The commentary revealed that these children had some understanding of sequential relationships. They thought about how one action can impact another action, and the overall sequence of how actions come together to make things work. You may not have words from children in your form if you are working with younger children or children who are quite focused and silent during an observation, but it is still valuable to imagine their internal thinking.

Focus on Differing Children's Perspectives

You may realize the diversity in your classroom more vividly when you begin to interpret from children's perspectives. Cultural perspectives from children's experiences enter their play in many ways. Value the opportunity to learn more along these lines.

Did You Look at the Events from the Children's Perspectives, to Wonder How They Experienced Things?

The strategy these preservice teachers used to think from the child's perspective was to record evidence from their observation record in the form of a child's statement and to reframe what the child said in the teacher's own words. The teachers were trying to enter the child's mind, processing events in the order in which the events influenced the child's verbal communication. For example,

> Ryan A.: Push the button. I know that when I push buttons, things happen. When I push the on button on the TV, it turns on. When I press the button on my toy, it moves.

Did You Describe and Question Unexpected Events that Indicate When Children See Things Differently?

Christina and Freda did not document an example of what might be considered a question or event that was unexpected. Even the questions around how the garbage makes electricity, which are unique for young children, were logical in relation to the video they saw explaining that the incineration process leads to a process involving electricity. To illustrate an unexpected event, we offer an example from the bluegrass study that was shared earlier in the book.

As you recall, when teachers realized that some children were aware that music can be read on a sheet of paper, they created an area for writing music and set out a set of colored handbells (representing one octave) and markers of correlating colors. Children were invited to write music that others could read and use to play music with the bells. Anji, a child from China, wrote a series of English letters in lines across the page and then invited a teacher to move her finger from left to right, in the direction English is read, across each line throughout. As the teacher

followed her instructions, Anji sang the entirety of "You Are My Sunshine." This was unexpected from a child who had not yet spoken more than a word or two at a time in English in the classroom. Teachers learned a great deal from this unexpected event about how much Anji was retaining from her classroom experiences. Anji's actions influenced other children to write music notations in a format that followed the formal mechanics of writing, and she inspired the teachers to provide provocations for music notation over many months.

Focus on Learning Opportunities in the Play

When you notice thinking and learning you want to support and extend, you are likely relating to children's play with the empathy needed for designing meaningful learning opportunities.

Did You Look Ahead to How Your Ideas Might Be Used in Planning?

As a whole, the incinerator narrative illustrated that children had a strong desire to make sense of how things work. It is clear that the preservice teachers had thought about and provided recycled materials to facilitate thinking about garbage. It is not clear from their statements that they were thinking ahead about materials to use as the project progressed. However, their clear indication of the directions of the children's thinking (e.g., creation of a functional conveyor belt, the end product of electricity) showed that they understood the concepts to plan around for further investigation.

Did You Articulate Various Hypotheses About Opportunities in the Play to Extend the Children's Development, Knowledge, or Understanding?

The teachers generated multiple hypotheses about the children's reactions to the garbage and the process (claw action, hopper, fire, ashes, electricity, and light) of turning garbage into energy and light. They listened as children expressed their interest in and knowledge of incinerators and paid attention to the details of the children's reasoning process.

Based on their hypothesis that the children wanted to understand the mechanics of the claw's movements, Christina and Freda planned for next-step learning opportunities with handheld claws that children could manipulate to observe the actions that make the claw move. Later, an interpretation from the exploration of the claws led Christina and Freda to plan an opportunity for children to further explore ways to control the handheld claws.

Did You Describe in the Narrative What You Saw or Heard that Led You to Your Ideas?

All speculations should be backed up by your evidence statements. Christina and Freda literally copied statements or descriptions of actions from their observation record and pasted them into the interpreting thinking form so they could see the relationship between what happened and what they were thinking about the events.

Did You Look Back and Ahead to See Whether You and the Children Are Pursuing Distinct Threads of Inquiry?

A Big Idea represented in this inquiry was to learn about the process of garbage disposal and incineration. There were many threads associated with this concept, each distinct but all related: what is the claw's job, what is the conveyor belt's job, what is the end product of the incinerator's work? Each interpretation demonstrated that the teachers were thinking of different ways to challenge, guide, and question the children to deepen their understanding of the topic.

For Further Reflection and Inquiry

On your journey with emergent inquiry you now have a tool for interpreting children's thinking to speculate and learn more about the children. Investing in time revisiting your observation records will energize you and lead you to better understand the meaning behind the details. Taking this time to reflect deeply helps you and your coteachers to prepare to be with the children in ways that intentionally guide their thinking in new directions. The many theories you've identified as you interpret will lead you to the next process of developing curriculum action questions, a turning point in the emergent inquiry planning process that is presented in Chapter 6.

For deeper reflection on interpreting children's knowledge and thinking, try these suggestions:

1. Think back on your week and the time you spent with coteachers. What was the focus of those shared moments? How might you intentionally plan to spend the same amount of time with teachers reviewing and interpreting observation records?

2. Look at the schedule of staff meetings. Can administrative information be shared in other formats, such as email, so that teams of teachers can spend staff meeting times revisiting and interpreting observation records?

3. Review the observations you have been documenting. Are there enough details stating the actions or dialogue for you to interpret a meaningful event? Do you need to revisit the observation record chapter to better develop your documentation skills?

4. After revisiting and interpreting observation records with a coteacher or teaching team, jot down your feelings. What kind of teacher have you become through this process?

5. How does learning about children influence your journey as a teacher?

CHAPTER 6
Developing Curriculum Action Plans

At this phase in the COI planning process, teachers begin to see their questions about children's strategies, goals, and theories as diverse threads of inquiry, representing the many paths the inquiry might follow. Teachers develop many questions through the process of interpreting children's play (Silveira & Curtis 2018). They find themselves questioning children's actions where the meaning wasn't clear (Wien & Halls 2018). They wonder how to support children in developing an understanding of certain phenomena. Unexpected events often catch teachers' attention in ways that make them ask why and how they occurred. For example, one day a boy chose to come up close to the camera with a prism over his eyes when his teacher was videotaping. She wondered, "Is he trying to see me from a new perspective, or does he want me to document his experience?" We will refer to this example throughout the next sections in this chapter to help you understand how these teachers used this videotaping experience to develop questions for their curriculum action plans. Through this sort of careful observation and interpretation, teachers also discover the many questions children ask directly, like "What makes the bike go?" or "Where does the rain come from?"

To "support children's genuine understanding" (Jones, Evans, & Rencken 2001, 27) of their world, consider which of their questions can be the source for the next steps in an emergent inquiry process (Wien & Halls 2018). Was the child with the prism thinking, "What will happen when I come really close to the video camera screen?" When the teacher interpreted this as a possible question the child held, she acted on her speculation by flipping the camera's LCD screen (it was an older video camera) toward the boy for him to explore further, empowering him to feel he was directing this experience.

Determining which questions can frame the ongoing inquiry so children feel they are agents in their own learning is difficult for even the most seasoned emergent inquiry teachers (McDonald 2019). Your next step for planning emergent inquiry curriculum is to document ways you might intervene—adding materials, asking questions or statements to provoke children's thinking, determining strategies that would encourage children to act on their thoughts. Look back at your interpretations of the children's play to explore a variety of different ways to challenge or question the children to extend their play into areas that represent what they experience as their own inquiry.

The COI Curriculum Action Plan form (see Appendix 3) asks teachers to list each of these challenges or questions along with relevant materials and statements or questions that could productively guide each as if it were to be the very next step in the learning process. Recording what children would need in order to explore and find answers to each action question is a goal of this form. As you begin to think divergently to consider the many possible directions and materials for supporting children's inquiry, you will generate several questions in relation to your interpretations of the nuances of children's thinking. Through this process you will develop a flexible mindset so that you can recognize, accept, and respond to the unexpected from children (Wien & Halls 2018) and allow the flow of the curriculum to follow the ideas that diverge from a more typical linear path. The many questions you develop continue the divergent thinking (brainstorming) processes that began with your interpreting thinking.

Mary Lee Martens (1999, 26) recommends using questions to focus attention; help children measure, count, and compare; encourage action; pose problems; and support reasoning:

- *Attention-focusing questions* help students fix their attention on significant details.

  Have you seen . . . ? What have you noticed about . . . ? What are they doing? How does it feel/smell/look?

- *Measuring and counting questions* help students become more precise about their observations.

  How many . . . ? How often . . . ? How long . . . ? How much . . . ?

- *Comparison questions* help students analyze and classify.

  How are these the same or different? How do they go together?

- *Action questions* encourage students to explore the properties of unfamiliar materials, living or nonliving, and of small events taking place or to make predictions about phenomena.

  What happens if . . . ? What would happen if . . . ? What if . . . ?

- *Problem-posing questions* help students plan and implement solutions to problems.

  Can you find a way to . . . ? Can you figure out how to . . . ?

- *Reasoning questions* help students think about experiences and construct ideas that make sense to them.

  Why do you think . . . ? What is your reason for . . . ? Can you invent a rule for . . . ?

The Role of Divergent Thinking in Emergent Curriculum Planning

Understand that the curriculum is your responsibility and the questions you pose drive the process along (McDonald 2019). A thousand questions come to mind in one day. You inquire to find something out. Children do too. When your speculations about what is going on in children's minds make you want to do something, to intervene, to act on these speculations and write down what you are wondering about when you want to intervene, then you have probably formed a good action question for developing curriculum. As you reflect on your questions, consider whether any Big Ideas link them together. Big Ideas of perspective and perception were developed by the teachers in the video experience with the boy with the prism, linking their action questions together into what they saw as potential for guiding long-term emergent inquiry curriculum. Their action questions are provided as examples in the section "Getting to Know the COI Curriculum Action Plan Form."

The action questions you pose determine the materials, setup, guiding questions or statements, and the procedures for the next intervention into children's play. Excellent teachers generate questions rapidly, documenting all so that each can be referred to for planning for immediate next steps and into the future. Through careful reflection you will then choose to explore one or two at a time, in depth, and then intervene in play for specific reasons. The teachers who were inspired by the video experience with the boy with the prism developed several action questions, each of which had the potential to facilitate different threads of inquiry. They reasoned that there was potential for learning related to the Big Ideas of perception and perspective as well as learning opportunities related to content standards.

- A question related to using visual perception through observing and drawing could align with math standards of proportion and size.

- A question for exploring and developing understanding of perspective in relation to the video camera could address technology standards.

- A question for learning more about the perceptions of others in the community ties into social emotional and social studies standards.

Action Questions

We have adopted the terms *action question* for use in the COI system after careful consideration of the many terms used across several sectors of the educational arena. There are many terms used in certain educational settings that do not carry over to other settings in meaningful ways. The use of this term is meant to bridge the cultures of early childhood education, early childhood special education, and research. When Reggio-inspired educators state that they are recording their "wonderings" (Gandini & Goldhaber 2001), a colleague in special education or educational statistics might not understand the link between the word and the teachers' serious questions for inquiry. Action questions imply that possible responsive actions can be taken.

Getting to Know the COI Curriculum Action Plan Form

Use the COI Curriculum Action Plan form to record the action questions you develop and related strategies for engaging children in their next steps for exploration and learning. This form asks you to record the tag for noting the relevant Big Idea or thread of inquiry, the observation date, and the interpreters' names. There are three rows and two columns. Action questions are inserted into the left column and in the column to the right of each is where you record what you need to facilitate that action question as if it were to be the next exploration session—materials as well as questions or statements to provoke and promote the inquiry.

The three rows in this form prompt you to develop at least three action questions, a minimum for thinking beyond your first thoughts for action. Add rows to the form or copy the form as needed for developing as many action questions as possible. This stretches your ability to think divergently, and divergent thinking is an effective tool for problem solving and planning (Chant, Moes, & Ross 2009; Duckworth 2006; Treffinger & Isaksen 2005). As you focus on Column I, consider that each action question is a possible proposal for the next play session. In a later step in the planning process, discussed in Chapter 7, you'll see the ways teachers synthesize their many action questions into an emergent inquiry curriculum plan.

Column I: Action Questions

Column I asks you to develop action questions related to an intention that might include one or more of the following:

- Questions you want to pursue about the children's thinking

- Things you think the children want to understand further or are stuck on

- Questions you have from the perspective of a researcher trying to learn more about the children in order to help them develop deeper understanding of the topic they are pursuing

- Questions that provide ample opportunity for incorporating materials and provocations related to early learning content and standards

Action questions prepared by teachers in response to the videotaping and prism experience are provided as examples with some of the related content links. These represent three of the teachers' early action questions in an emergent inquiry curriculum that followed many twists and turns over the course of one school year:

- Can children learn more about experimenting with their actions in relation to a video camera and TV monitor?

  › Language arts content links: vocabulary; explore and describe a wide variety of objects and their attributes

- Math content links: listen to and use comparative words to describe the relationships of objects to one another

- Technology content links: make predictions about changes in materials or objects based on past experience

■ If we surround a portrait subject (e.g., toy bear in a chair) with a wooden frame, will children only reference what is in the frame when they observe and draw, or will they include what they see outside the frame? Will they think about what is near and what is far away?

- Math concept links: explore and describe a wide variety of objects and their attributes; shapes; spatial relationships

- Technology content links: record observations and share ideas through simple forms of representation such as drawings

- Art content links: line; shape; observing; use of drawing materials; visual representation of what they see or know

■ Can we explore ways that others (peers, toy bear, adults) perceive with their eyes, ears, senses, feelings?

- Math content links: explore and describe a wide variety of objects and their attributes (as children explore with eyes, ears, hands)

- Social and emotional content links: relationship skills; social engagement; social awareness; communication

Column II: Provocation Strategies

Column II asks you to record a list of the materials, productive questions, and statements that you think will guide the children's investigation and theorizing in relation to each action question—that is, what you would provide and say to facilitate inquiry around that action question as a possible next session with children. These ideas are the basis for the teacher-initiated and responsive provocations that you will organize into an inquiry provocation plan, which is explained in Chapter 7.

Provocation strategies related to the action question from the previous section are listed below. Remember that they focus on Big Ideas of perception and perspective.

■ Materials and questions or statements to support the question about experimenting with a video screen that was linked to a TV monitor

- Materials:
  - Video camera on a tripod connected to a monitor
  - Video camera hooked up to projector facing the screen
  - Objects of interest for children to create a possible scenario and manipulate on the screen: toy bear, toy horse, children's bodies, other?

- Prompt questions:
  - Can you move the toy bear so you can see it on the monitor?
  - Can a friend who is viewing the monitor help you control what you do to make the bear visible on the screen?
  - What do you notice when you move close or far away or to the right or left of the video camera?

■ Materials and questions or statements to support the question related to the portrait-drawing provocation of a toy bear posed within a wooden frame. Will the child draw only the bear or include other objects in the environment?

- Materials:
  - Paper on an easel near subject, with pencil and eraser
  - Subject setup of a toy bear in a chair posed within a wooden frame

- Prompt questions:
  - Can you draw what you see through the frame?
  - Can you draw what you see that is near?
  - Can you draw what see surrounding the bear?
  - Can you draw what you see outside the frame?

- Materials and questions or statements to support the question for experimenting with diversity in perspective and ability. One child is blindfolded and led by another child to a particular center in the classroom where she is to explore with her hands.

  > Materials:

    • Scarf to use as blindfold for one child at a time

  > Prompt questions:

    • Can you identify which learning center you are in when blindfolded and escorted by a friend?

    • When you don't use your sight, what senses will you use to learn where you are in the classroom?

Considerations for Your Intervention Strategies

The primary considerations that will provide guidance and meaning to your process include preparing for conversations, asking productive questions, providing materials, incorporating new materials, and researching content. Each of these considerations is examined below.

The process of developing provocation strategies is complex. Thinking divergently and innovatively to guide children's inquiry so that next steps in developing curriculum will seem meaningful and linked to previous play is a creative and sometimes intuitive process. You need to consider the ways that conversations with children can inform the trajectory of their ongoing inquiry, or just what makes a question or statement productive for inquiry, as well as when it might best serve the forward movement for you to create materials for the next steps in an ongoing process. You can gain a lot of insight into the children's thinking by understanding when it would be helpful to ask children to represent their thinking with new materials. When you face content that is unfamiliar, reach out to experts in the community to reinvigorate the learning process for yourself and the children. All of these strategies surface repeatedly in teachers' work with emergent inquiry curriculum planning and require further discussion in the following sections.

Preparing for Productive Use of Conversations

As they interact with materials and peers, children discover problems, pose questions, and discuss their working theories with others who provide essential feedback for moving experiences and thinking forward. The divergent thinking that is generated among a group stimulates children to continue on and to test their theories in ways that won't occur without the input of peers (Chant, Moes, & Ross 2009; Duckworth 2006; Treffinger & Isaksen 2005). In these instances, children are explorers who are deeply engaged within their play to the extent that they might not differentiate play from investigation.

This excerpt from a conversation among children in the process of propping up a curtain like a tent in their outdoor playground is a great example of a conversation where divergent thinking (the many ideas of peers) productively moves the play along. Notice how the ways they interact with the materials are also a part of their conversation. Each child has new ideas to add to the process.

Mrs. Sally: How are we going to keep the tent up?

Sara: A pole.

Morgan: Paper clips.

Sophia: Maybe some tape.

Mrs. Gloria: (*Leaves the playground and returns with five bamboo sticks, a tin filled with paper clips, and a roll of masking tape.*)

Micah: We need another stick.

Gerry: We need to bury the stick in the ground. (*Gets a shovel from the sandbox and begins to dig holes to put the sticks into.*)

Peter: (*Comes over to see what is happening.*) What game are you playing?

Group: We are not playing. We are making a tent.

Gerry: (*Continues to dig holes for the sticks.*)

Group: (*Place the sticks into the holes.*)

Mrs. Sally: The sticks are not standing up. How can we help them stand up?

Cindy: Get another stick.

Mrs. Sally: I have tape. Will the tape work?

Group: (*Work to connect the sticks using the tape.*)

Mrs. Sally: It is still falling down. What else can we do?

Gerry: We need another big stick.

Stephanie: It's breaking. (*Tries to reposition the tape and puts more dirt around the sticks.*)

Gerry: (*Gets some buckets and fills them with sand, then places the sticks in the buckets.*)

Children develop conversation skills when they are allowed to initiate major components of a conversation with ideas that are innovative to them and free of adult coercion. You can encourage this autonomy by being present as a listener during conversations and by observing to know when to offer provocative questions or statements. Documenting conversations in writing shows the children that what they say matters and provides you with more evidence of children's ideas. In classrooms where children are used to teachers transcribing their conversations, they will likely seek out a teacher when they are about to engage in a meaningful discourse because they want the teacher to record the event. These children eventually realize that teachers use these records to plan with and for the children.

Use the COI Curriculum Action Plan form for designing intentional conversations to learn more about a process that previous documentation has not yet clarified. Plan for conversations that invite a few new players or the whole class into the thinking of a group as a way of providing feedback or generating new ideas. As you learned previously in the chapter, begin by developing an action question or introductory statement to frame the discussion. Formulate several questions or statements to have ready as supports for extending the conversation once it is underway. Consider any materials that might assist children in focusing on the content of the discussion, like photos of their work or materials they are exploring that can be touched and used within a group in an exploratory and informative way. For example, consider a teacher presenting children with the book *If I Build a Car* (by Chris van Dusen), which

focuses on unique features of vehicles. She prepares statements: "If you were to build a car, what would be the most important parts to include?" and "Can some of us take turns to share ideas on the purpose of one of these car parts?" She also provides large photos of boats, cars, and airplanes for children to look at for comparison questions and statements as preparation for eventually drawing blueprints to build a car.

Allow for space and time for children to work with the materials and discuss the possibilities. When questions are targeted to the children's purposes and materials are available to focus and guide their thinking, children can take the lead in conversations so you can sit back, observe, and document, inserting reflective statements to reinforce or questions to extend.

To generate a discussion about what a group of 3-year-old children notice along roads, teachers invite children and families to bring in items or photographs of items they found on the road. The content is meaningful to children, as they are constructing a large road in their classroom, and the concrete materials will help to focus their thinking. A teacher takes photos of the lines on the road outside the school and in the parking lot, of the street signs at the corner and in the parking lot, of the train track that runs along the road across the street from the school, and of the signs along the tracks. She has enough images for each child to hold one.

The conversation begins with a statement and then a question as the teacher hands each child an image printed to the size of an 8.5" × 11" piece of paper. "Take a close look at the picture I gave you," she says. "Can you tell me what you see?" This group of young 3-year-olds becomes engaged in a lengthy discussion, reviewing and presenting from different perspectives, a process that also prepares them to then watch with wonder as one peer empties a bag full of sticks and stones and discarded items that were collected from along the roadside on a walk with a thoughtful parent. Through careful preparation, the teachers are able to experience for the first time a situation in which all children are voluntarily a part of the conversation for about a 20-minute period with no distractions.

As each child shares, the teachers are able to sit back, observe, and insert reflective statements to mirror back to the children their own ideas or to clarify meaning. Teachers also tests or challenge children's working theories with productive questions like "What does that (stop sign) mean?" and "How do you know it means to stop?"

Considering Productive Questions and Statements

Productive questions and statements are not easy to formulate. Emergent inquiry teachers want to plan for ways to elicit children's ideas (Wien & Halls 2018), a process often in great contrast to their own early learning experiences where teachers were the ones asking questions and expecting specific responses. To go beyond this call-and-response approach that is still prevalent in many early childhood classrooms (Engel 2011), teachers must dissect the many functions of questions and use them in ways that encourage children to reveal their own understanding of the world (Rosenthal 2018). Open-ended questions leave room for diverse responses, yet teachers must learn to go further using questions and statements and materials to build around the main focus of the conversations (Silveira & Curtis 2018).

Consider the reasoning for your questions, as recommended by constructivist educators (e.g., DeVries et al. 2002). You might do one or more of the following:

■ Learn more from the child. In the example below of the shadow from the child's hand, if the teacher asked, "What is that shape?," the teacher might learn something the child knows—if the child can name it as a shadow. In contrast, asking "What do you see?" might lead to learning other kinds of thinking from the child, such as the way the shadow moves or changes with the movement of the hand.

Using Productive Questions

In the photo shown here, the teacher carefully watched a child play and wondered, "Does she think that shadow is paint? She acts like she does." The teacher waited and watched and eventually decided to do something to find out. He asked, "Is that paint?" He waited a bit as the child looked at the shadow and then touched it. The teacher then made a competing shadow with his own hand and ask the child to make a prediction: "What would happen if we covered that spot?"

The teacher had observed carefully, speculated about an interest and question on the part of the child, planned a couple of ways to challenge the child to consider her own thoughts and actions, and intervened by enacting his plans. When teachers use the COI processes of observing, documenting, reflecting, and planning, they are developing the habit of mind of a researcher. The teacher is researching how a particular child takes in the world, interprets it, and acts upon it. Teachers develop competency with these practices that can be used on the spot as well as for long-term planning.

Exploration of the shadow of a hand

- Challenge children's current thinking. In this example, the teacher challenged the child's thinking with a question that might defy the reality but still seemed plausible: "Is that paint?" The question challenged the child to reconsider any previous ideas about shadows and possibly test out this theory by touching the shadow to feel if it was paint. This type of interaction encourages language and interaction with materials while promoting a higher level of reasoning.

- Pose questions that involve a choice. Choices such as "Do you want to work on the airplane project or read a book?" assist children in making decisions that will benefit them.

- Ask questions that help children to think about their own thinking. You can ask how to accomplish particular tasks or how a particular action or process occurred: "How did that ball going down the tube score a point in your game?"

- Ask questions to provoke children to show their thinking. Providing new materials to guide children's responses is also helpful. For example, give a child a marker and paper to show how the ball scored a point. Asking a child "Can you show me how the worm moves?" can elicit lots of interesting movements from children that can connect to the reasons the worm moves (e.g., for shelter, to dance, because it is giggling).

Providing Teacher-Created Materials

Many educators think that project work means that children should make all the materials for an exploration. Sometimes it may be the teacher's role to create materials to guide the inquiry further. For example, in the bluegrass study, teachers learned early on that the children were aware that people who play instruments are in bands. Children eventually began to talk about how bands perform on stages. To learn more on their thoughts about bands and performing, the teachers decided to create a stage with mock instruments (refer back to Chapter 1). They realized that if they were to ask the children to make a stage, they would be redirecting the children away from their real focus of performing. Stage making would lead to a lot of thinking about construction when it appeared that the children really wanted to perform. Therefore, teachers

created the performing stage. Consider very carefully when the children's inquiry will most benefit from teacher-created materials.

Representation and Re-representation

The concepts of representation and re-representation are used brilliantly by Reggio Emilia educators to reveal and extend children's working theories, modeling problems and solutions in much the same way as scientists (Forman et al. 1998; Schaefer 2016; Weatherly, Olesan, & Kistner 2017). Representation refers to the initial way a child expresses an idea. This could be through talking, drawing, or enacting, among other expressive forms of communication. Re-representing refers to the child expressing the idea in a new form, which could be talking, drawing, enacting, and so on. Each time a child re-represents a particular idea, the new material affords different opportunities for elaboration (Schaefer 2016). There are so many materials children can use to express their thinking, which Loris Malaguzzi identified as the hundred languages concept (Edwards, Gandini, & Forman 2012).

A favorite example for understanding these concepts comes from teachers who facilitated the build-a-car project. Children represented their early understanding of cars in drawings, which then led to creating model cars from clay. They were also invited to use their bodies to represent the movement of cars and wheelbarrows, which helped them make sense of the relationships between the more complex car and the simpler mechanics of the wheelbarrow. All of this incorporated several discussions, representing children's developing thinking through verbal conversations and ideas about design through drawing. A final form of re-representing their ideas about cars was the process of collaborating to locate loose parts, items they thought would be useful to construct a large prototype of a car. This process of re-representation is key to extending projects over longer periods of time; from each representation new ideas emerge that suggest new directions for learning and discovery (Schaefer 2016).

Incorporating New and Innovative Materials

Reggio-inspired educators have also shared their brilliance in the use of innovative materials for guiding inquiry. Natural materials are an essential tool for exploration in emergent inquiry classrooms (Schaefer 2016). Children can use a branch or tree cookies (slices of tree trunk) to symbolize in as many ways as they might do with blocks. Choosing open-ended materials allows children the freedom to think about the materials' functions in ways that match their current purposes (Silveira & Curtis 2018). The provision of open-ended materials doesn't assure that children will engage in deep inquiry, however. The choice of materials and their presentation will frame the way the children approach and use them. Consider materials that are new and innovative but relate in some way conceptually to the theorizing and purposes of children (Baker & Davila 2018; Schaefer 2016).

Stove made from loose parts

A good example is found in the process of constructing a stove for a mud kitchen. Children in one classroom were provided with a large box, a variety of paper products, and different types of cardboard materials, including egg cartons that they used as stovetop burners. After looking at a photo of a stove and drawing a blueprint, the provided materials were easily organized into a model of a stove.

The children, however, noticed a problem: "This can't go out into our mud kitchen because it's only cardboard." They knew the limits of cardboard when left out in the elements. Thus, this model became their prototype for theorizing about new materials to create a sturdy structure for their outdoor kitchen. They chose wood because they knew it was strong. Circular loose

parts were provided, such as reels from an old movie projector, which proved to make more realistic burners than the egg cartons, whose shape is quite different from that of actual burners. Children rummaged through the many metal components from computers, parts of wire shelving units, and other metal materials to discover a perfect shelf for the interior of the stove, round components to represent knobs for turning burners off and on, and a metal towel rod that they transformed into the handle for the door of their stove. Their teacher intentionally sought out and provided children a variety of metal and wood materials that held the potential for representing parts of the stove.

When to Research Content

Children often become very interested in topics that teachers are not familiar with. Welcome these as opportunities to grow with the children. Investigation is essential for successful co-inquiry with children. Generate dialogue with children to enlist their ideas about how to learn about a topic, where to go to learn about something, and who to ask. Listen carefully and record their responses and insert your own ideas as a participant with the children. Then to go to the places the children suggest, seek out the people they recommend, and find the materials they need to move an investigation forward. By engaging and following through, you are modeling the inquiry process for children (Baker & Davila 2018).

Many early childhood teachers feel a sense of excitement when encountering the unknown. They are ready to dig into research and exploration (Baker & Davila 2018). Others, however, encounter a sense of discomfort, a lack of control or authority when facing the unknown. It takes courage to ask questions that lead to researching content and discovering approaches for study that diverge from simplistic textbook activities. When teachers find and present misleading information, like creating a baking soda explosion and referring to it as a volcanic explosion, they do a disservice to children who might be seriously invested in the workings of real volcanoes.

The questions and searching processes you encounter with children may lead to dead ends, leaving you uncertain as to where to go next. These are important moments to dig deeper and seek assistance from experts in the field. Consider when it is best to tackle the research for a while, independent of the children, to learn enough to guide the processes with children.

Consider when and whether an expert you locate can share information in ways that children will be ready for or receptive to, as in the following example.

A group of children are paying close attention to marks in the dirt outside, which they begin referring to as animal tracks. They wonder what the animals were and where they came from and went. One of the classroom teachers meets with several local experts to experience firsthand what they have to offer prior to inviting any to visit her classroom. There is a very kind Audubon guide who has a sheet with diagrams of animal tracks and a lecture with great images of animals from all over the world. However, his lengthy talk doesn't allow for interaction or questions until the end, so he doesn't seem a good candidate for engaging young children's attention.

Instead, the teacher invites an outdoor adventure guide from a local center because his presentation would engage children interactively while also answering some of their questions, eliciting discussion, and generating new questions. He provides charts for each child illustrating tracks of local animals that children might see in their backyard or in the wilderness in their region. He also shares wonderful photos of these animals. He uses a sandbox and rake for his presentation to guide the children through a process of thinking about and predicting what the tracks of each animal might look like. Then he uses his own body to mimic the movements of bears, rabbits, and other animals in the sandbox, raking the sand between each example.

Children are then invited to model his movements to make the tracks themselves. This leads them to think and talk about the ways each animal moves through the environment, to imagine these animals' encounters with trees and foliage given the way each animal moves, and to imagine and research the power of the front and back legs of rabbits, how high a rabbit can hop, and how a bear walks on two legs to eat leaves from high trees.

Similarly, in the bluegrass study, two experts were asked to participate throughout the entire study. Both were musicians who played in bluegrass bands. They were available to share real instruments with children, provide information to teachers about the physics of sound, locate songs to incorporate into the study, and more. These individuals were present in the classroom over time, developed real relationships with the children, and became part of the classroom community.

Using the COI Curriculum Action Plan Form
Learning from the Incinerator Project

The COI Curriculum Action Plan form example in this section is from Christina and Freda, and represents three cycles of their long-term emergent inquiry project. We'll summarize to refresh your memory of this project. The COI examples we share begin with children viewing video of an incinerator, an interest that emerged prior to our example when children questioned where the trash goes. The functions of the incinerator observed in the video fascinated the children and were explored in discussion around the video and an experience with bags full of trash, used to see if children could re-represent the structure of the incinerator they learned about in the video. The second provocation was to experiment with handheld claws to better understand the function of the incinerator's claws, and the third provocation was to look even more closely at the handheld claws by taking them apart with a screwdriver.

The process of developing action questions leads to the generation of many questions, each of which can be explored in some way over the course of a long-term emergent inquiry investigation. As you proceed beyond this stage in planning, you will discover that you might design a next-steps plan that incorporates facets from several of the action question ideas you've developed.

Christine and Freda chose to revisit their cycle 1 action questions each time they moved on to a new cycle. So, instead of seeing three COI Curriculum Action Plan forms, you will see how this team *added* to their original thinking on their initial form, using red for the additions in their second cycle and blue for additions in the third cycle (see Figs. 6.1 and 6.2). Read on to learn how the forms developed by Christina and Freda align with criteria noted in the COI Curriculum Action Plan Checklist found in Appendix 3.

Tag:
Researchers: Christina Raffoul and Freda Shatara

Date:

EXPLORE WHAT YOU WANT TO PURSUE WITH THE CHILDREN
This is divergent thinking. Be creative but stay grounded in your observations and speculations about the children's play. Looking back at your interpretations of their play, explore different ways to challenge, guide, or question the children to extend their play into the areas you think they are working with. These can become the emerging threads of the curriculum you are developing with the children.

Column I—Action questions: You develop your curriculum from questions you want to pursue about children's thinking or things you think the children want to understand. **Below, write 3 or more questions you could act on to develop threads in your curriculum. You are not creating a sequence of sessions. Each question represents one next possible session with children.**	Column II—Provocation strategies: You guide the curriculum by provoking thought—by providing opportunities and experiences that deeply engage the children, draw forth their competencies, and build mastery. **For each action question in Column I, record the materials and productive questions or statements you will use to guide a next play session centered on your action question. List the many diverse materials, along with several productive questions/statements, that will help children experiment with and extend their theories.**

1 What are the parts/process of the incinerator?	1. Work with a K–W–L chart to see what children are most interested in learning.
	2. Look at pictures of incinerator as a whole and point out the different parts
	3. Printed images of incinerator
	4. Video of incinerator from previous sessions
	5. Revisiting questions
	  a. What is the claw's job? How does the claw work? What else are claws used for? (in other settings) (relates to cycle 2; relates to cycle 3)
	    i. Look at the small claw from a closer perspective and break it apart to see the parts. How do the parts connect together to open and close it? How is this like the bigger claw?
	    ii. How do the controls on the claw move?
	  b. What does the burner/furnace look like? What is the burner/furnace's job? Where else do you see burners/furnaces?
	  c. What does the conveyor belt look like? What is the conveyor belt's job? Where else do you see conveyor belts?
	  d. Tall chimney (where smoke comes out at the end); What does the tall chimney look like? What is the tall chimney's job? Where else do you see tall chimneys?
	  e. Discuss the process of the incinerator

2 How can you represent the incinerator?	1. Draw each part of the incinerator
	  – Pencils & thinking pens (thin point felt markers)
	2. Build the parts of the incinerator
	  – Small blocks
	3. Build the incinerator as a whole
	4. Draw the incinerator as a whole
	5. Provocation questions

Figure 6.1. Curriculum Action Plan form for the incinerator project.

3	What are recycled materials?	1. Discuss what a recycled material is (in general). Recycle vs. Non-recycle; Paper vs. plastic; Trash and Recycling; How long does the process take? Sorting with Venn diagrams; Picture cards
		2. How can you sort recycled materials? (Use for Cycle 3 with handheld claw)
		3. Bring in recycled materials from home to be sorted during class (represented by a chart) (Use for Cycle 3 with handheld claw)
		   a. Begin recycling in the classroom using bins
		4. Provocation questions: (Use for Cycle 3 with handheld claw)
		   a. What is the recycle process? What are the steps in recycling? How do recycled materials become something new? How is each material recycled differently?

4	What is electricity?	1. Group time about prior knowledge of electricity (K-W-L chart)
		   a. Where does electricity come from in the incinerator process?
		2. Provocation questions and statements
		   a. How does electricity work? Conservation. What makes the lights go out?
		3. Electric circuits
		   a. Series
		   b. Parallel
		   c. Creating circuits
		   d. Exploring wires
		   e. Insulators
		   f. Conductors

5	Exploring food as a recycled material. What is compost?	1. Work with K-W-L on ideas about composting at school
		2. Videos on composting
		3. Books on composting
		4. Provocation questions
		   - What is compost?
		   - How can we compost from our classroom/school?
		   - What happens to food when composted?
		   - Where do we use compost?
		5. Draw ideas about composting
		   - Paper and thinking pens

Check for Big Ideas. Before you begin planning, reflect on the questions you are pursuing with the children. Pull in the standards. From your perspective as a "knowledgeable other," do you see a bigger picture forming? Jot it down here.

The Big Idea for this inquiry is collaboration/problem solving. We are integrating this Big Idea with the children's interest in incinerators.

Figure 6.2 Curriculum Action Plan form: The Incinerator Project (continued).

From Children's Interests to Children's Thinking

Column I: Exploring Hypotheses and Questions

What you insert into Column I represents questions that can help you learn more about children, what they think and understand, and what their purposes are. You might also include questions that you think the children might have, what they want to know and explore, or what they have already asked.

Do Your Action Questions Pursue or Speculate on Your Better Understanding of What Children Might Want to Know, Gaps in Children's Knowledge, a Child's Theory, Observed Problems, or Limits to Children's Thinking?

Christina and Freda quickly identified the children's interest in garbage disposal and incineration from their interpretations of the children's play. They tried to bring more information to the children regarding how the incineration process works. The five action questions addressed gaps in the children's knowledge and attempted to increase their understanding of recycling. The questions focus on the whole process of recycling, including the general recycle concept, incinerator machine operation, and representation of how an incinerator works.

Will Your Questions Lead Children to Pursue Their Own Questions and Theories?

Christina and Freda asked the following questions:

- What are the parts and processes of the incinerator?

- How can you represent the incinerator?

- What are recycle materials?

- What is electricity?

- What is compost [exploring food as a recycled material]?

Four out of the five questions start with "what," which indicates the teachers' desire to pursue children's own questions about the recycling topic and other components related to the children's interest in incinerators. The second question about representing the incinerator would help the teachers facilitate the children's own theory development with graphic (drawing) representations that could also reveal the children's ideas about how an incinerator works.

Do Your Action Questions About Recent Play Connect with Earlier Play?

All five action questions seemed to connect with earlier play about the claw/grabber and how it works. The children mentioned that they were wondering about the claws and how it picks up the garbage and its movements. Christina and Freda developed these five questions after revisiting previous COI Observation Record and Interpreting Thinking forms. They were building on earlier play with the intention of guiding children to learn more details about how an incinerator works and to explore the components of the recycling process.

Do Your Action Questions Facilitate Children to Revisit and Re-Represent Their Previous Experiences and Learning?

One of the five questions focused on the facilitation of drawing, building, redrawing, and rebuilding children's representations of an incinerator. The plans revealed an intentional teaching and learning progression through exploration, representation, and re-representation.

Will Your Action Questions Engage Children in Collaboration with Peers and Adults as a Community of Learners?

All five questions were intended to invite a small group of children to pursue them. The observation and interpretation is based on the small core group of children.

Did You Discover a Thread of Inquiry Among a Small Group that Can Be Explored with the Whole Group?

The plan was intended to involve the whole class with many different components of the recycling concept. Threads were small concepts (e.g., how does a trash moving claw work?) that built an understanding of the entire concept of trash disposal and incineration. Questions that drew children in pursuit of threads were present; Christina and Freda tried to learn what children know of the parts and processes of the incinerator, and one question linked to a thread about recycled materials. However, the connection from small group work to whole group discussion was not apparent in this curriculum action plan form. Thinking about such links will not appear in every cycle.

Do Your Action Questions Link Together into a Multifaceted Exploration of One Big Idea?

These preservice teachers researched the children's interest in an incinerator and how it worked and proposed many dimensions on this topic in which children could work together to understand these components. Each action question was generated from the children's interest. Christina and Freda observed collaboration among children, which led them to develop a Big Idea of collaborating to solve problems, and they linked this to the Big Idea of incinerators. Thus, Christina and Freda were planning around content that developed social skills as well as the understanding of science concepts related to the incinerator.

Column II: Developing Provocation Strategies

Column II is where you insert your ideas for materials, questions, and statements that can productively facilitate each action question from Column I. Think of each row (action question and provocation strategies) as a possible plan for your next session with children. Develop three or more rows of action questions and strategies to stretch your thinking and to consider what might be the best possible next step for the children's inquiry. So, you are really thinking of many possible next-step ideas. These are not meant to be a list of plans to move through in a sequential order. Instead, when you move on to the next part of the COI planning process, you will ideally synthesize your many action questions and strategies in a way that incorporates ideas from each into an inquiry provocation plan.

Do Your Provocation Ideas Focus on the Questions You Posed for Each Action Question?

Christina and Freda recorded lists of provocation strategies that were diverse and detailed. Their questions focused on a whole process of recycling, including the general recycle concept, incinerator machine operation, representation of how an incinerator works, and learning about electricity.

Their provocation questions and statements focused on the detailed steps and information needed to facilitate each action question they proposed. In relation to the first action question, the teachers asked, "What are the parts/process of the incinerator?" It seemed that the teachers considered identifying the parts and process of the incinerator an important first step in building further understanding about how an incinerator works. This is a pedagogical learning experience that Christina and Freda tested out in order to understand how children learn. This inquiry process is about studying the children's theory first and the facts later, a reversal of many conventional teaching methods.

The second provocation plans focused on the children representing the incinerator in drawings and three-dimensional constructions. This back-and-forth process guided the children's inquiry toward new knowledge construction as each new representation generated new questions. The third and fourth provocation plans also corresponded well to the action questions.

Did You Introduce or Shift the Materials so that They Afford Increasing Exploration for Children to Make Their Thinking Visible, Better Understand Their Ideas, Gain New Perspectives, and Learn Properties of the Materials?

The materials included pictures of incinerators, videos of simple machines, and recyclable items for sorting as well as discussion activities about electricity as a means of promoting children's understanding of the recycling process. These divergent provocation strategies demonstrated a direct connection to the teachers' observations and interpretations that children wanted to understand how incinerators work and what occurs in the process of trash disposal.

In this plan, identifying the parts and process of the incinerator was an important first step in building further understanding about how an incinerator works. To guide their first action question, Christina and Freda prepared by having pictures of incinerators available to identify the different parts (e.g., claw, burner/furnace, conveyor belt, tall chimney) and to discuss the process of incineration. They planned to revisit the incinerator video to discuss the workings of the incinerator and help children draw connections between simple machines and the incinerator parts. Under the second action question, the children were asked to draw and build each part of the incinerator and then build the incinerator as a whole. These plans revealed the teachers' ideas for increasing exploration to make children's thinking visible through their expressions with materials.

Did You Plan Statements that Might Provoke Conversations Among the Children to Further Explore Their Thinking During New Play?

While Christina and Freda designed many productive questions to facilitate children's learning, in this particular planning cycle their ideas for productive statements were not present. Productive questions move the conversation forward, drawing out children's thinking so that children can drive the bulk of the conversation or experience autonomously. By including discussions as a part of each provocation for learning, it was clear that these preservice teachers valued children's conversations in the learning context.

Christina and Freda included a statement for directing their facilitation, which could actually be verbalized to children as a productive statement because it had the ability to move children to action: "Look at the small claw from a closer perspective and break it apart to see the parts." Another possible productive statement for guiding the process of drawing or enactment might have been "Show me what you think are the different parts of the incinerator."

Did You Plan Guiding Questions to Facilitate Conversations Among the Children to Further Explore Their Thinking and Pose Their Own Questions During New Play?

The provocation questions started with "what" and moved toward "how" in relation to the specific action questions. The sub-questions showed a balance between presenting facts in open-ended ways in conjunction with questioning and materials exploration as a means for knowledge construction in children's learning.

The provocation questions were multifaceted, provoking further inquiry on many aspects of the overall topic of incinerators and trash disposal. The questions were designed to ask the children to come up with their own interpretations of the processes they were investigating. Some questions suggested explorations that could help children to make sense of the concepts related to a recycling process. The following questions demonstrate the teachers' intention to further explore the children's thinking: What is the recycling process? What are the steps in recycling? How is each material recycled differently?

For Further Reflection and Inquiry

Observe, interpret, plan, intervene with a provocation is a pattern for the COI planning process. When you follow this pattern, your practice is a lot like a researcher's, studying with children and about children. This requires thinking on many levels about strategies that use divergent thinking. The goal is to design future learning experiences that have continuity with the children's thinking and prior experience. This phase of the COI planning process takes time that is worthwhile. When you organize ways to accommodate for this planning time, ideally in collaboration with your coteacher or teaching team, this deep intellectual work takes you far beyond the role of curriculum deliverer or classroom manager. You are transforming your speculations into questions that frame the plans for provocations for children's play in order to investigate the effects. You will experience being a co-researcher and co-learner with children, engaging in intellectual work together (Edwards, Gandini, & Forman 1998; Hill, Stremmel, & Fu 2005; Stacey 2009).

For deeper reflection on developing questions and a curriculum action plan for your classroom, try these suggestions:

1. As you go through the next week, notice and document the experiences where you want to learn more regarding what the children are thinking about what they are doing.

2. What are your questions about learning during these experiences? Do you question children's misconceptions about a topic or whether children are ready to progress to a more complex experience of a topic?

3. What do you think children might be wondering about when they explore during these experiences?

4. Ask your coteacher to observe and document in the areas where you have documented what children are doing so he can develop his own questions. Then compare your questions to gain insights from each other's perspectives.

5. As you develop questions about children's experiences, notice when you are forming hypotheses about what children might be thinking. Then you can begin to distinguish the difference between interpreting children's thinking and developing questions about their thinking.

6. Videorecord children in a learning center and observe your recordings with your colleagues to collaboratively develop action questions.

CHAPTER 7
Planning and Implementing a Provocation

This chapter guides you to consider the ways that all of the previous COI processes (observing, interpreting, and developing curriculum action questions) influence your COI Inquiry Provocation Plan (see Appendix 4). Previous phases called for divergent thinking; here you will think convergently so you can narrow the many diverse ideas you've generated into a plan to pursue with children. Recommendations for implementing your provocation plan are also discussed in this chapter.

The attention you give to observing, interpreting, and wondering about the needs and thinking of children is equal to the thinking you invest in your planned provocations—the materials you put out, the way you put them out, what you say or ask, and the way you speak. All lead children's thinking and actions in particular directions. As an adult, you come from outside of the children's peer culture. Therefore, you will plan very intentionally to guide children's emergent inquiry along lines that remain as close to the children's thinking and peer culture as possible. Provocations—which are modifications to the environment that involve your entry into children's play, a restructure of learning groups, or a shift in materials—change children's play, explorations, and investigations. Exploring children's thinking can lead to many ideas for you to intervene systematically to support the children's inquiry in ways that children feel are natural extensions of their experiences.

Emergent inquiry curricula are curricula because they follow a reasonable flow. They are pulled forward naturally toward some attraction to uncover meaning for the children *and* the teachers. The curricular processes may go in different directions, so that not all children are following a single thread. For example, in the bluegrass study several children engaged in

the processes of pretending to be performers, others became very focused on writing music notation that peers could play with concert bells and handbells, and another group of children spent time exploring the instruments and their sounds.

The threads move children forward toward their interests, which might change as different groups of children encounter slight modifications or circumstances. With thoughtful, deliberate planning you can guide the smooth flow of these divergent threads of emergent inquiry curricula.

When planning a provocation, consider the following:

- Why are you intervening?

- What are you trying to accomplish or help children accomplish?

- How will you use your resources?

- How will you enter and withdraw from the children's activities to help them learn and master what they need to know?

Thinking About Children's Conversations and Representations when Planning Provocations

It's likely that you are interested in emergent inquiry curriculum because you want to actively engage children in their environment, provide them opportunities to form goals, discover how their internal representations of things do or do not work, help them wonder and be puzzled, and explore further with them when they want to know something. You can facilitate this learning by inviting children into experiences where they must represent their own thoughts with a variety of materials and by generating authentic conversations with them about their thinking and goals. You'll develop your ability to plan for conversations that generate discussion among children. You'll also learn to notice the meaning of a conversation of sorts between a child and the materials he is using. For example, Roger had been exploring ways to incorporate all the clay tools he could manage to set into his clay structure (below). The sticks, spoons, and knives the teacher provided as clay tools became functional parts of his clay castle. He was likely envisioning each as a tall tower.

Michelle adds water and spreads it around. She adds more water and uses the knife to continue to spread it more. "It [the clay] is melting."

Roger is using all the tools. He has not left one out of his structure. "It's a castle."

Michelle's conversation with materials was her focused process of adding clay to the tin of water and then adding more water. She also used a plastic knife to spread the clay to make a smooth surface across the top of the tin (top right). As she noticed the clay slip out of the can and onto the table, she said, "It is melting." She may have been thinking of the clay in relation to her knowledge of ice or snow, something that can transform from a solid to a liquid.

Allison, the teacher presenting these clay provocations, was inspired by the children's use of clay in books she read about Reggio-inspired explorations (Smith & Goldhaber 2004; Topal 1998). With little previous experience, she bravely introduced clay, clay tools, and water, leaving the children to explore with many materials, undisturbed time, and little guidance. She was not sure what to expect or how to work with clay, but she was deeply motivated to observe and document so she could learn from the children's experiences. Each child approached the clay, the numerous clay tools, and water with a different mindset. Children didn't recognize the many materials as clay tools but used them *with* the clay as structural building materials. Allison documented the children exploring the properties of the clay, the tools, and the way water affected the clay.

It was not clear that the children would make a curriculum on their own to challenge and extend their thinking about the properties of clay, of tools, or of the effects of water on clay or of clay on water. On their own, young children are likely to draw naïve conclusions from their experiences. While the

From Children's Interests to Children's Thinking

children were motivated and involved with the clay as presented, the fascination of mixing clay and water and combining the clay with the existing materials might well fade without Allison and her coteachers guiding the children to look at the clay in new ways and explore multiple threads of inquiry with the clay. Their guidance could eventually lead children to master the basic skills of manipulating clay for explicit representations. To do this, Allison and her coteachers chose to refocus children by reflecting on her documentation, forming action questions and provocations, and synthesizing these ideas into an inquiry provocation plan for helping children learn more about the properties of clay and different approaches for exploring clay, with or without tools.

Focusing to Keep Children Engaged in Intellectual Work

What drives the curriculum forward is planning for opportunities where children's questions are just out of reach or their interests are slightly inaccessible. Is the clay really melting? Can the child recognize the transformability of the clay without tools or water? When you form questions like this from your observations, you realize that children's goals require a little something more, that they are confounded somewhat, or that their theories of the world are incomplete or unsatisfying (DeVries et al. 2002; Duckworth 2006). You need to plan for experimentation with the materials that challenges and advances children's knowledge and thinking.

In the clay example, Allison and her coteachers found that this brief experience led children to form theories about clay and clay tools that held great potential for diverse threads of inquiry, including (1) exploring clay without tools or water, (2) exploring clay with minimal tools, and (3) working from a large piece of clay versus many small pieces. Since children used the tools as parts of their building structures, Allison and her coteachers imagined that

a new presentation of clay without tools or water would facilitate an approach for manipulating the clay with hands, an idea children might not otherwise have considered. They organized this plan in the COI Inquiry Provocation Plan form based on their thinking about the early observations of the children's clay exploration that Allison documented in the first three COI forms (observations, interpretations, and curriculum action questions).

These teachers were inspired by the children's response to this new presentation, interpreting the lack of talking as a sign of meaningful "dialogue" with the clay as the children constructed theories about the ways that their actions (e.g., pounding, rolling, pulling pieces off, pinching) transformed the clay (see the photos below and on the following page).

Sophie pulls off small pieces and attaches them to form structures.

Roger discovers many ways to manipulate the clay, including using his elbows to pound it.

The twin goals in designing an emergent curriculum are to follow the thinking, needs, and interests of the children closely and yet to move into situations where children need to grow and work to be satisfied. In the clay example, the children remained engaged while focusing on a new approach with the clay. Before returning to this example, let's take a look at the COI Inquiry Provocation Plan form and how it can help you achieve both of these goals.

Getting to Know the COI Inquiry Provocation Plan Form

On the COI Inquiry Provocation Plan form (see Appendix 4), you revisit your observation records, interpreting thinking records, and action questions to design emergent inquiry curriculum plans that stay close to the children's thinking while provoking extensions. *Your* thinking about the *children's* thinking is the rationale for designing next steps in the

emergent inquiry curriculum that you record on this form. This form has several sections in which you will document the specifics of the plan for your next steps.

You will develop a question with a rationale and then focus on three elements for designing a provocation: materials, setup, and questions. Choose materials for the opportunities they offer children to explore and theorize. Consider how to set up the environment so that, as much as possible, the materials alone will invite the children to explore in ways that ask less of the adult and more of the children. Ask yourself whether the children will know what to do without asking for assistance. You will also think about the many productive questions you might use to facilitate new thinking and questioning among the children as needed. The goal is to interact productively with as little interruption of their focus as possible.

This overall process involves convergent thinking, a term from creativity theory that describes the process of narrowing your many divergent ideas into the one that has the most potential for going forward. As with the previous COI forms, you will note the tag as the related Big Idea or thread of inquiry that the plan is following, in addition to recording the names of the planners, the children you will invite to participate, and the area, date, and time for the planned experience.

Action Questions: Keep Your Intentions Clear

To move children's play toward focused intellectual engagements, you will plan to explore questions. It's important to be explicit about whose questions are guiding the provocation. It could be your question about the children or a question the children present. You will develop the guiding question for your inquiry provocation plan by revisiting your action questions. You may choose one of those questions or restructure one or more into a new question.

Ground Your Plan in Your Observations and Speculations About the Children's Thinking

This section of the form ties your action question to your theory about why the question is important to children in relation to evidence from play you've observed.

Rationale

Look back at your COI Observation Record memos and your ideas about children's thinking recorded on the COI Interpreting Thinking form, and use these to write a rationale that states why you are pursuing the action question (or questions) you chose for your plan. This grounds your plan around children's thinking.

Evidence

You should be able to pinpoint evidence from your observations that grounds your inquiry provocation plan in the thinking of children. Highlight observation details from across the play situations you have documented and copy these selections into the evidence section of the COI Inquiry Provocation Plan form. This evidence represents your reason for your plan. This objective data must be copied exactly as stated in your observation record (i.e., names, actions, words).

Big Idea: Check for Big Ideas

You want to identify a Big Idea focus for your inquiry provocation plan. Remember that your action questions represent possible threads of inquiry for exploration. Your Big Idea is a core framework that links together several emerging threads of inquiry (Chaille 2008). Revisit the discussion of Big Ideas in Chapter 3.

Big Ideas can remain consistent from cycle to cycle in this COI process or they may be tweaked in ways that align with the Big Idea in previous cycles. Record your Big Idea for your plan in this section.

Design the Provocation

As you design your provocation, you will experience the significance of thinking ahead about the specific materials and setup, as well as the questions or statements you might pose with children to guide the implementation of next steps in the inquiry process. You will feel well prepared for the implementation.

Materials

Choose materials for their affordances and their ability to provoke theory building in the children. Consider whether the materials are new and require time for learning more about their particular properties and possibilities. If the materials are familiar, are they just the right choice for the next steps in the inquiry? Will the children be fluent enough to use them for the intended purposes? Is some minimal form of open-ended modeling necessary, a process that will suggest ways to appropriately work with the materials while inspiring the children to work independently and divergently? Is it a reasonable time to introduce a familiar material for a new purpose?

Also, consider if the materials can align with the concepts that are the focus of your inquiry provocation plan. Recall the example in Chapter 6 in which a teachers found that the round shape of the reels from an old film projector guided children's thinking more toward a functional burner on a stove than the egg cartons provided for the initial cardboard stove they created. Also consider if it is necessary to consult an expert (e.g., a painter, scientist, dancer, musician) to determine just what might be the best choice of materials.

Setup

Write a description of how you will set up the environment so that the materials will guide the children. You have the ability to arrange the setup within the learning environment in ways that open and extend children's activities or constrain them. You want them to know how to enter into the experience with minimal adult intervention. When modifying the environment, consider the materials you intend to use from several perspectives: the child's and your own view of how the materials work, the opportunities they might afford a child, how the qualities of the materials might invite exploration, and how presenting materials in unusual ways might highlight new ideas about their properties and confound children's theories in ways that give them new ideas. When you describe the setup specifically enough for a substitute to understand, you will have mentally prepared yourself to facilitate this provocation.

Questions

In this section you will record the many questions or statements you might use to productively facilitate thinking and learning around the concepts identified in your plan. Developing these questions and statements doesn't necessarily mean you will use all—or even any—of them with the children. Too much probing and prodding can actually stifle a child who is focused.

You will rely on these questions or statements as needed, when there is an opening in which the children are likely to be receptive to your interacting in ways that empower them to maintain a sense of autonomy in their process. Designing these questions ahead of time prepares you for the unexpected that will inevitably arise from children as they engage in an open-ended, nonlinear process and allows you to follow with them as their questions lead you all in new directions.

Outline Your Procedures and Number the Steps

This is a valuable section of the COI Inquiry Provocation Plan form. It prompts you to think ahead about how you will introduce the children to the provocation. What do you think children will do in the area you have prepared? What processes will encourage them to formulate questions and goals and follow their goals? What forms of documentation will best capture the experiences? Some recommendations for procedures include these:

■ Hold a focused discussion with a small core group and encourage children to revisit previous experiences or dialogue about new content.

■ Use a focused meeting with the whole class, revisiting the work of a small core group to introduce new ideas to peers, who can in turn provide feedback.

■ Invite children to explore the materials in a center, set up in ways that inspire them to form questions and goals related to the materials and that provide you with new information about their understanding of the materials.

■ If an appropriate time, invite children to use materials to represent their thinking about a concept.

■ Document with a video or audio recording or photos and written records. Children's creations, such as drawings or sculptures, might also serve as documentation.

These are just some of the many strategies you might use. In this section of the form you will also state how you will document the play so that you can revisit the experience for future planning. Write the procedures clearly so that another teacher can reasonably follow them.

Using the COI Inquiry Provocation Plan Form
Clay Exploration Example

The following section guides you through the use of the form in relation to the clay example introduced previously in the chapter.

Action Questions: Keep Your Intentions Clear

To begin, Allison and her coteachers returned to their COI Curriculum Action Plan form, where their questions related to the ways they perceived children were thinking about clay in their first experience. These experiences included children filling containers with small pieces of clay, using tools as building structures, experimenting with consistency of clay using water, and incidentally working the clay with their hands. The teachers noted these actions questions:

1. Can the child mold with a larger body of clay or build with small pieces?

2. Would the child be interested and able to construct something in clay without tools?

3. Do the children know these are tools designed for specifically manipulating the clay? Can we help children to become more thoughtful in their use of clay tools?

4. Can we help children be more aware of the impact of water in constructing with clay? How important is water for working with clay?

These action questions reveal these teachers' overarching focus on what might happen if the children did not have clay tools or water and how to help children learn more about the function of tools and water when working with clay. From this perspective, you can see that Allison and her coteachers did not merely choose one of their action questions to guide their inquiry provocation plan but converged the ideas from more than one question into two new questions to provoke children's next steps with clay:

- What can children learn about clay when they are not provided tools or water?

- In what ways can they manipulate the clay using just their hands?

Ground Your Plan in Your Observations and Speculations About the Children's Thinking

Allison backed up her action question with a rationale that she borrowed from her COI Interpreting Thinking form and related evidence from children's play that she copied from her COI Observation Record form.

Rationale

Allison and her coteachers pulled their rationale from their interpreting thinking form, linking their thinking about the observation with the new direction of their plan:

> We saw the children using all the tools in so many different ways, even using them as structural materials instead of tools. This made us think that we did not provide them an opportunity to explore the clay with their hands. So, we want to provide clay for them again with fewer tools, so that they can explore with their hands.
>
> We also saw the children using a lot of water. We think that they were most interested in using all the materials we provided, checking out what each can do. We want to limit the materials we provide so that they can explore the clay with more focus on the clay itself.

Evidence

This evidence from their COI Observation Record form linked to the questions and rationale Allison and her coteachers designed:

> R: Is using all the tools. He has not left one out of his structure. "It's a castle."
>
> S: Picks out pieces of clay and puts them into the funnel until it is filled.
>
> J: Fills a tuna can and uses a knife to scrape across the surface. "I made a cake." Finds a new tool, a small plastic rake, and begins to rake across the clay in the tuna can, watching how it makes marks in the clay.
>
> m: Adds water and spreads it around. She adds more water and uses the knife to continue to spread it more. "It [the clay] is melting."

Big Idea: Check for Big Ideas

Allison and her coteachers believed their Big Idea held their action questions together as a curricular framework that would allow for pursuit of new and related thinking:

> Exploring the language of clay through aesthetic and artistic approaches and the use of tools that help deepen the children's understanding of the clay's properties and potential for expression.

Design the Provocation

Allison was prepared to facilitate her inquiry provocation with children with a clear knowledge of the questions she would pose and a sense of how the materials would guide the children's inquiry process.

Materials

Allison and her coteachers outlined all the materials needed to facilitate children's inquiry around their two guiding questions, noted previously.

> **materials:** Four sizeable clumps of clay presented in different ways for each of four children, boards for working on with clay, water out of sight but on hand in case it is needed.

Setup

Setting out the clay in four different shapes invited children to touch and manipulate it, and their ensuing deep engagement left little need for talking among the group or the teacher's facilitation. Allison was able to stand back and observe, recording with the COI Observation Record form and photographs. The setup of the materials and a simple statement by Allison, "Show me what your hands can do with the clay," guided children to make their own connections to new concepts in ways that were tightly linked to their previous play experiences. Here is Allison's setup:

> Clay will be presented on four boards, so that each will guide just one child to each board. Each board will be placed in front of one of four chairs at the table, which will also be a visual cue for "one child per board." Each board will have clay presented in a different way: a flattened piece, a clump, a tall cylinder shape, a coiled shape.

Allison described the setup of the materials clearly enough that another teacher could organize the experience if she were absent. She considered the way children would "read" the purpose of the center by taking the time to mold the clay in a variety of ways to provoke diverse approaches for clay manipulation, and the one-to-one matching of chairs to boards with clay suggested that four could work at the table.

Questions

Allison prepared these questions and statements:

- Show me what your hands can do with the clay.

- What are you doing to manipulate the clay?

- How many different ways can you manipulate the clay?

- What will you do with
  › A slab of clay?
  › A hunk of clay?
  › A tall cylinder of clay?
  › A coiled piece of clay?

Outline Your Procedures and Number the Steps

Allison and her coteachers listed their procedures with numbers, outlining an overall developmental process for this inquiry experience that is open ended and encourages children's autonomy:

1. Invite children to manipulate the clay with this prompt: "Show me what your hands can do with the clay."

2. Guide the children to consider as many ways as they can to manipulate the clay.

3. Encourage the children to discuss their processes together as they work with the clay.

   a. Share new strategies with peers.

   b. Share ideas about products with peers.

   c. Share problems with materials with peers.

4. Observe and document carefully throughout the experience.

5. If children stop or seem stuck, or if there is an opening to share a new approach with the clay, guide as needed with the modeling of materials or with conversation or questions.

6. Document with a camera and written observation record.

Using the COI Inquiry Provocation Plan Form
Learning from the Incinerator Project

There are three sets of COI Inquiry Provocation Plan forms for the incinerator project shared in this section, one for each of three COI cycles (see Figs. 7.1–7.6). These examples highlight the ways in which Christina and Freda addressed the criteria within the COI Inquiry Provocation Plan Checklist that is provided in Appendix 4. The planning in the COI Inquiry Provocation Plan form builds on Christina and Freda's COI Observation Record forms, COI Interpreting Thinking forms, and COI Curriculum Action Plan forms. Christina comments on the relevance of this form for planning:

> " In the Inquiry Provocation Plan, I had to ground my thinking and look into what the children may be thinking. I think the speculation on children's thinking is a major part of this inquiry planning as it is throughout the COI inquiry process. In this section, I had to show why I was going the direction I was going in the inquiry with evidence from the children's actions and words. I think this gave credibility to the lesson as well as helped me hold myself accountable for my reasoning. I was able to show why I was thinking something based on the children's speculated thinking. I was also able to revisit the Big Ideas and questions I had for the children each time I created an inquiry, and this was a good way a keep me on track with the purpose of the lessons.

Cycle of Inquiry
Inquiry Provocation Plan

IPP

Tag: Incinerator Project—computer and drawing
Planners: CR and FS

Date: For Jan 27

BRING YOUR IDEAS INTO A PLAN
This is convergent thinking. Use the ideas you've generated from thinking about the children's play to create a planned intervention. Use enough details in each box so that another person could set up and guide the play session that you are planning.

AREA: Carpet area for inquiry
PARTICIPANTS: Two small core groups
DATE & TIME: Tuesday (1/27) and Thursday (1/29) PM Explorations

---

ACTION QUESTIONS: Keep your intentions clear.

Revisit your action questions. Which question or questions are you pursuing?
Do you see already see a clear thread emerging in the play?

What are the parts/processes of the incinerator?

GROUND THE PLAN IN YOUR OBSERVATIONS AND SPECULATIONS ABOUT THE CHILDREN'S THINKING.

RATIONALE: Look back at your observations, memos, and interpretations. Write an interpretation that states why you chose to pursue this action question with children.

The children have been interested in incinerators. We previously watched a video that gave an overview of the process and a few children were able to recall events that occurred. We wanted to revisit this video, so more children had the opportunity to view it and retain the information. We wanted to introduce them to a K-W-L chart and fill it out according to the video and what we would be exploring the rest of the semester.

EVIDENCE: Revisit the OR form and copy selections that pinpoint the actions and words that helped you formulate your question.

I learned that it turns into steam.

We're going to make an incinerator. I want to make a grabber. (Pointing to bottles) These move to the fire.

(Pointing to plastic container) This can be the grabber. This is what it looks like. (He put it through the conveyor belt.)

(Put garbage in the grabber, pretending to pick it up)

Okay, it's on the hopper on the conveyor belt. Here is a pile of ash after it goes in the fire. (He and Ian put garbage all over the conveyor belt.) Now all of this is turning into ash! There's a lot of garbage turning into ash.

Big Idea
Check for Big Ideas. Before you begin planning, reflect a minute about the questions you are pursuing with the children. Do you see a bigger picture forming? Try to see the ways that any of the threads you identify remain consistent from cycle to cycle. If you see a way they link together in any way - you likely have identified a Big Idea/s. Note your thoughts here.

The Big Idea in our classroom is problem solving and collaboration. We are integrating this Big Idea with the children's interest in incinerators. In this lesson specifically, the children are thinking about what they want to learn and discussing thoughts, opinions, and predictions with one another to form conclusions.

Figure 7.1. First page of the COI Inquiry Provocation Plan form for cycle 1 of the incinerator project.

BRING YOUR IDEAS INTO A PLAN
This is convergent thinking. Use the ideas you've generated from thinking about the children's play to create a planned intervention. Use enough details in each box so that another person could set up and guide the play session that you are planning.

DESIGN THE PROVOCATION. Align this with the questions you are pursuing with the children.

MATERIALS: Choose the materials for their affordances and their ability to provoke theory building in the children.

- Computer
- Video previously watched (Link is on the drive)
- Word document
- Paper
- Thinking pens (thin point felt markers)
- Small blocks and bricks

SETUP: Design the play environment to be the third teacher and to invite the children to explore. Write a description of how you will set up the environment so that the materials will guide this play session.

Chairs will be set up around the computer (4–5 children at a time). The left screen will be used for the word document, for the K–W–L chart, and the right screen will be used to view the video.

After watching the video or on a following day, children will then be invited to draw what they know about incinerators at small group tables. Tables will have paper, thinking pens, and small piles of small blocks and bricks at each seat.

QUESTIONS: Think ahead about **the many** productive questions you might use when you interact with the children during their play.

In chairs with video and chart:

- What do you remember from the video?
- Did you learn anything new from the video?
- What would you like to learn about incinerators?

At small tables with drawing materials:

- Show what you know about incinerators.
- What is that part of the incinerator called?
- Show how the conveyor belt moves.
- How does ash turn into steam?
- What is steam?
- Show what you remember about recycling.

OUTLINE YOUR PROCEDURES. Number the steps 1, 2, 3, etc.

How will you introduce the children to your provocation? Will you start with a focused small core group discussion or a focused classroom meeting with the whole class, invite children to explore the materials in a center, invite children to represent their thinking with the materials, enter into a dialogue with the children? These are some of the many strategies you might use. Think through what you will do, including **how you will document the play** so you can evaluate what happened and plan from it. Write your procedures so that another teacher could reasonably follow them.

1. During group time, tell the students that they will be looking at the incinerator video again and seeing if they can remember things from the first time and learn new things from it.
2. The children will sit in the chairs by the computer and be introduced to a K–W–L chart. ("We're going watch the incinerator video, but first we want to show you a new kind of chart. We're going to look at this spot today and try to remember what we already know about incinerators.")
3. The children share what they know, and what they want to learn and are still wondering about incinerators. ("What else do you remember from the video? Did you learn anything else from the explorations we've done? What else do you want to know about incinerators? I'm going to write your ideas here. Do you want to know about a certain part?")
4. The children will watch the video and answer/ask questions during.
5. After the video, children will talk about what new things they have learned to the person sitting next to them, and as a whole, we will talk about what they learned. ("What did you and your partner talk about?")
6. The children will transition to a different investigation. …. And then ….Repeat steps 1–8 with each group of children.
7. Following this group discussion invite children to drawing table.
8. Ask children to show what they know about incinerators, the process and how they work.
9. Interact with appropriate questions as needed.
10. Collect drawings as additional documentation, along with video, photos, and written observation records.

Figure 7.2. Second page of the COI Inquiry Provocation Plan form for cycle 1 of the incinerator project.

Tag: Incinerator Project—exploring claws
Planners: CR and FS

Date: For February 3

BRING YOUR IDEAS INTO A PLAN

This is convergent thinking. Use the ideas you've generated from thinking about the children's play to create a planned intervention. Use enough details in each box so that another person could set up and guide the play session that you are planning.

AREA: Block area
PARTICIPANTS: Open
DATE & TIME: Tuesday (1/27) and Thursday (1/29) PM Explorations

ACTION QUESTIONS: Keep your intentions clear.

Revisit your action questions. Which question or questions are you pursuing?
Do you see already a clear thread emerging in the play? What are the parts/processes of the incinerator?

GROUND THE PLAN IN YOUR OBSERVATIONS AND SPECULATIONS ABOUT THE CHILDREN'S THINKING.

RATIONALE: Look back at your observations, memos, and interpretations. Write an interpretation that states why you chose to pursue this action question with children.

After conducting the first inquiry with the children, the main focus was the claw/grabber and how it works. We want the children to have the opportunity to explore how a claw opens and closes. They will be using hand-held claws to observe this motion and to get a sense of cause and effect when they push on the lever and it moves. Eventually, the children will explore taking apart the claw and investigating the parts and how it moves, but that will be a separate lesson.

EVIDENCE: Revisit the OR form and copy selections that pinpoint the actions and words that helped you formulate your question.

- I know that the claw goes down and picks it up and it drops it.
- I remember the grabber that swings, and it picks up the recycled bottles. The grabber goes up and down and up and down.
- I don't know how the claw moves.
- I am wondering about the claw and how it picks up the garbage.
- I am wondering about how the claw works.

Big Idea

Check for Big Ideas. Before you begin planning, reflect a minute about the questions you are pursuing with the children. Do you see a bigger picture forming? Try to see the ways that any of the threads you identify remain consistent from cycle to cycle. If you see a way they link together in any way—you likely have identified a Big Idea/s. Note your thoughts here.

The Big Idea in our classroom is problem solving and collaboration. We are integrating this Big Idea with the children's interest of incinerators. In this lesson specifically, the children are focusing on the claw/grabber and how it works and is able to pick things up.

Figure 7.3. First page of the COI Inquiry Provocation Plan form for cycle 2 of the incinerator project.

BRING YOUR IDEAS INTO A PLAN
This is convergent thinking. Use the ideas you've generated from thinking about the children's play to create a planned intervention. Use enough details in each box so that another person could set up and guide the play session that you are planning.

DESIGN THE PROVOCATION. Align this with the questions you are pursuing with the children.

MATERIALS: Choose the materials for their affordances and their ability to provoke theory building in the children.
 	
 • Hand-held grabbers
 • Recycled materials of various sizes
    – Bottle caps
    – Bottles
    – Cans
    – Plates
    – Paper towel rolls
	SETUP: Design the play environment to be the third teacher and to invite the children to explore. Write a description of how you will set up the environment so that the materials will guide this play session.
	
	 In the block area, the materials will be set up on the floor after group time. The claws will be in a basket for the children to explore.
		QUESTIONS: Think ahead about *the many* productive questions you might use when you interact with the children during their play.
		
		 • How are these like the big claw from the incinerator?
		 • How do you think it opens and closes?
		 • How can it pick things up?
		 • Where are you going to put the object after you pick it up?
		 • How does the big claw open and close?
		 • What do you think is inside the claw?

OUTLINE YOUR PROCEDURES. Number the steps 1, 2, 3, etc.

How will you introduce the children to your provocation? Will you start with a focused small core group discussion or a focused classroom meeting with the whole class, invite children to explore the materials in a center, invite children to represent their thinking with the materials, enter into a dialogue with the children? These are some of the many strategies you might use. Think through what you will do, including **how you will document the play** so you can evaluate what happened and plan from it. Write your procedures so that another teacher could reasonably follow them.

Provocation: During group time, tell the students that we will be exploring the hand-held grabbers and looking at how they work like the big claw of the garbage incinerator.

1. Once the children come to explore the investigation, we will observe how they interact with the materials on their own.

2. As the children explore with the materials, we will promote discussion by asking questions about how the claw works. ("How do you think the claw works?" "Why does it move the way it does?")

3. We will also ask the children how the claw opens and closes and take note of their observations and inferences. ("How do you think the claw opens and closes?" "What do you notice about the way the claw opens and closes?")

4. As they explore with the claw and how it opens and closes, we will discuss what they notice about how it picks up the materials and moves them to a different place. ("How can the claw/grabber pick things up?" "Where are you going to put the object after you pick it up?" "Is it easy or hard to pick things up with the claw/grabber? Why?")

5. After the children explore with how the claw moves, we will bring up the idea of what the claw is made up of inside and have the children make predictions. We want them to focus on cause and effect and how certain parts of the claw cause it to move in different ways, which is the effect. ("What do you think the claw is like inside?" "How does this part make the claw move in a certain way?"—We will point to different parts and ask the same question. We will also ask, "What do you think will happen to the whole claw if I move this part?").

6. We will go over the questions and review how the claw works and how the children can make connections between the hand-held claw and the garbage incinerator claw. We will also encourage discussion among the children, so they can talk about their observations and ideas with each other. For example, we might say to a child, "Watch how this person uses the claw to grab the recycled materials. They are being slow and steady with the claw, so they don't drop the object."

7. If we notice a child is having trouble using the claw and picking up the objects, we will encourage them to ask their peers around them for help. ("Instead of asking me, why don't you ask that person to help you? I'm sure they will help you pick up the object.")

8. Each time new children arrive at the area, we will encourage the children who are already there to explain to the new children what they are doing with the claw and recycled materials. We will also suggest that the new children ask questions of the children who are already there, just like in step 7.

Documentation will be taken in the form of video, pictures, and written observation records.

Figure 7.4. Second page of the COI Inquiry Provocation Plan form for cycle 2 of the incinerator project.

Tag: Incinerator inquiry project—close look at claws' functions
Planners: CR and FS

Date: For February 10

BRING YOUR IDEAS INTO A PLAN
This is convergent thinking. Use the ideas you've generated from thinking about the children's play to create a planned intervention. Use enough details in each box so that another person could set up and guide the play session that you are planning.

AREA: Kitchen table during group time
PARTICIPANTS:
DATE & TIME: 2/10

ACTION QUESTIONS: Keep your intentions clear.

Revisit your action questions. Which question or questions are you pursuing?
Do you see already see a clear thread emerging in the play?

What are the parts/processes of the incinerator?

GROUND THE PLAN IN YOUR OBSERVATIONS AND SPECULATIONS ABOUT THE CHILDREN'S THINKING.

RATIONALE: Look back at your observations, memos, and interpretations. Write an interpretation that states why you chose to pursue this action question with children.

As the children were exploring with the small claws, we began to discuss how they work and what makes them open and close. We wanted to give them the opportunity to investigate what is occurring in the inside of the claw that makes it close when they squeeze the lever.

EVIDENCE: Revisit the OR form and copy selections that pinpoint the actions and words that helped you formulate your question.

- When you push down, it opens and closes.
- This metal thing. It goes through it. Then, it closes.
- I squeeze it together.
- When you put it up, it closes.
- Open, close, open, close. The claw is picking up (transferring).

Big Idea
Check for Big Ideas. Before you begin planning, reflect a minute about the questions you are pursuing with the children. Do you see a bigger picture forming? Try to see the ways that any of the threads you identify remain consistent from cycle to cycle. If you see a way they link together in any way—you likely have identified a Big Idea/s. Note your thoughts here.

The Big Idea in our classroom is problem solving and collaboration. We are integrating this Big Idea with the children's interest in incinerators. In this lesson specifically, the children are focusing on the claw/grabber and how it it works and is able to pick things up.

Figure 7.5. First page of the COI Inquiry Provocation Plan form for cycle 3 of the incinerator project.

BRING YOUR IDEAS INTO A PLAN
This is convergent thinking. Use the ideas you've generated from thinking about the children's play to create a planned intervention. Use enough details in each box so that another person could set up and guide the play session that you are planning.

DESIGN THE PROVOCATION. Align this with the questions you are pursuing with the children.

MATERIALS: Choose the materials for their affordances and their ability to provoke theory building in the children.
- Hand-held grabbers/claws
- Screwdrivers

SETUP: Design the play environment to be the third teacher and to invite the children to explore. Write a description of how you will set up the environment so that the materials will guide this play session.

The activity will be set up on the kitchen table during group time. The screwdrivers will be brought in by Ms. Raffoul and Ms. Shatara.

QUESTIONS: Think ahead about *the many* productive questions you might use when you interact with the children during their play.
- What do you think is inside of the claw?
- How are you going to open it to find out?
- What does that part connect to?
- Look at the bar, how does it move when you push on the lever?
- How does the claw/grabber open and close?

OUTLINE YOUR PROCEDURES. Number the steps 1, 2, 3, etc.

How will you introduce the children to your provocation? Will you start with a focused small core group discussion or a focused classroom meeting with the whole class, invite children to explore the materials in a center, invite children to represent their thinking with the materials, enter into a dialogue with the children? These are some of the many strategies you might use. Think through what you will do, including **how you will document the play** so you can evaluate what happened and plan from it. Write your procedures so that another teacher could reasonably follow them.

Provocation: During group time, tell the students that we will be exploring the hand-held grabbers and looking at how they work like the big claw of the garbage incinerator.

1. Predict how the grabbers are able to open and close. ("How do the grabbers open and close? What happens when you press on the lever?")

2. Discuss how the grabbers can be opened. ("What can you use to open these? What are some tools that may help us?")

3. Work together to unscrew the screws connecting the pieces together. ("What way do you need to turn the screw? How can you work together?")

4. Explore the inside of the claw. ("What do you see? What are all of those different parts? How do they connect together?")

5. Investigate how the claw opens and closes by observing what happens on the inside when the lever is squeezed. ("What is happening when you squeeze the lever? What is moving on the inside? How does this make it open and close?")

6. Relate the new information to how the claw of the incinerator opens and closes. ("How do you think this is like the claw of the incinerator? What do you think is inside of it that makes it move?")

Documentation will be taken in the form of video, pictures, and anecdotal notes.

Figure 7.6. Second page of the COI Inquiry Provocation Plan form for cycle 3 of the incinerator project.

Framing the Implementation by Aligning an Action Question with Evidence of Children's Thinking

Aligning your action questions with evidence of children's thinking, which ties together your interpretations (theories about children's meaning) and your observations, validates your plan. The next sections help you to link your plan to your observations by learning from the ways Christina and Freda's example aligns with the criteria in the COI Inquiry Provocation Plan checklist. If you post your plans in your classroom where families, administrators, and others can see them, you are helping them understand the reasons for what is occurring in your classroom and your intentions for guiding learning.

Did You Design an Action Question by Revisiting and Reframing Your Action Questions in the COI Curriculum Action Plan Form?

Christina and Freda chose to pursue one of five action questions. They continued to focus on this question throughout the three cycles represented in this chapter. Their action question, "What are the parts and process of the incinerator?," seemed to resonate most with the children's ideas.

Did You Pinpoint Evidence in Your COI Observation Record Form Directly Related to Your Action Question?

Their evidence in their COI Observation Record forms shows that Christina and Freda guided the children to make connections about how the claw/grabber works. Their questions were open ended and received many responses reflecting children's interest and new knowledge: children noticed the steam from the incinerator, the parts of the incinerator (claw), and the way the claw opens, closes, and picks up and drops trash.

In each COI Inquiry Provocation Plan form, the teachers could have noted the names of the children alongside their statements to identify and invite the children whose thinking was framing this plan into the provocation implementation.

Did You Develop a Rationale Linking Your Thinking and Reasoning About Your Action Question(s) to the Children's Thinking?

In their rationale for cycle 1, Christina and Freda stated that their main focus was to learn more of what the children knew and wanted to learn about the incinerator and how it works (using a K-W-L, or Know-Want to Know-Learned, process). In each rationale, you can see that Christina and Freda planned a trajectory with possibilities for teachers and children to work together in many ways, and they included information about materials they would use to guide the experiences and thinking. Each cycle moved the inquiry along in increments, each adding a twist to the opportunities for children to discuss and represent their thinking about the incinerator.

Did You Include a Big Idea that Links this Provocation to Previous and Possible Future Provocations?

Christina and Freda wove together their goals for guiding new thinking with children's specific interests and experiences from previous experiences. Their Big Idea statements represented a classroom culture of collaboration that they had witnessed and facilitated, and each cycle led to a next—cycle 1 to learning in cycle 2, and so on. Thus, the teachers were thinking ahead to future cycles as they planned.

Inquiry Provocation Plan: Materials, Environment Setup, and Productive Questions and Statements

The information you record in these sections prepares you to facilitate your plan effectively. By organizing the materials, setup, and questions or statements you will use, you are becoming very familiar with your plan. This way you can enter into the process with the children with confidence.

Did You Choose Materials that Afford Increasing Exploration for Children to Make Their Thinking Visible, Work Toward a Better Understanding of Their Ideas, Gain New Perspectives, or Learn Properties of the Materials?

Again, listing all the materials ensures you have thoroughly considered how they can help children experiment with and represent their theories. In the first cycle of the incinerator project, two computers allowed children to focus on more than one aspect of the incinerator at a time and compare and revisit throughout their discussion. The teachers also documented what children said, which helped the children recognize that their ideas were valued. In cycle 2, using the trash and handheld claw grabbers in a large open area inspired the children to work cooperatively to construct their own incinerator conveyor belt while learning about the function of the claws. The simple presentation of the handheld claws and screwdrivers built on the children's keen interest in the claws, allowing them to explore based on their question about how the claws opened and closed.

Did You Design a Way to Set Up the Materials that Will Invite Children to Play and Guide Them in Their Play so that Teachers Do Less and Children Do More?

The placement of materials for each example invited specific actions with the materials and interactions among children, keeping them quite engaged. The carefully designed setups allowed the teachers to sit back and observe the children's actions with minimal intervention.

The teachers could have included the number of chairs they would set up so children could clearly see the number invited to the inquiry. The K-W-L chart demonstrated to children that recording their comments during the conversation was significant to the teachers and helped the children understand that documentation represents their intended thinking and purposes. If you choose to use video, it can be viewed with children later to inspire them to discuss their many questions and theories.

The teachers chose an open floor space to set up the exploration of handheld grabbers as an extension of children's previous experiences and questions. The setup had the potential to encourage the children to test their theories so they could learn more about the claw's movement and how it worked. The placement of recycled materials in baskets was aesthetically pleasing and organized. The large space visually communicated that several children could explore the materials at the same time. The open-ended nature of the provocation encouraged collaboration.

The setup at the kitchen table suggested to children a more intimate arrangement at a height where they could get a close look at the materials that they would investigate and disassemble. The handheld claws and screwdriver provided an opportunity for children to develop theories and questions in the context of real tools. There was no mention of chairs, so the assumption was that there could be as many children at the table as could fit. If this was not accurate, then the teachers would need to list some method by which children could be aware of the limitations, such as the provision of four chairs.

Will Children Be Able to Read Your Presentation of Materials in a Way that Shows Them How to Enter and Respond in Relation to Your Action Question?

The first setup was a small core group discussion where it was clear to children that sitting together to view the computers was intended. The second provocation, drawing the incinerators, might not have been as clear to children without teachers' prompts, an important consideration when planning. There is not much needed for the children to then move right into the process of exploring with the handheld claws and using the trash in the open area to spontaneously decide to create an incinerator conveyor belt. In the third provocation, the screwdrivers and handheld claws clearly directed children's thinking toward taking apart the claws.

Did You Design Questions or Provocation Statements that Will Lead Children to Pursue Their Own Questions and Theories?

The questions Christina and Freda design were open ended and built on each other in relation to (1) the parts of an incinerator, (2) the relationship between the claws and recycled materials, and (3) how the claws worked. The close alignment of these concepts framed plans for extending the thinking observed in the children's play. Their teacher questions prepared them to assist children to think about their own actions in relation to the immediate feedback they got from the materials and peers during play. The planned questions showed an intentional sequence for guiding children's thinking.

It is important to remember at this point in your planning that these questions are not designed to bombard children during their conversations. Ultimately, you want the materials to inspire a discourse among children that will build as independently of your intervention as possible. Hold your planned questions to use at just the right time, if necessary, to prompt the children's thinking to incrementally move forward.

Cycle 1:

- What do you know about incinerators?
- What do you remember from the video?
- What is that part of the incinerator called?
- How does the conveyor belt move?
- How does ash turn into steam?
- What is steam?
- What do you remember about recycling?
- Did you learn anything new from the video?
- What would you like to learn about incinerators?

Cycles 2 and 3:

- How are these like the big claw from the incinerator?
- How do you think it opens and closes?
- How can it pick things up?
- Where are you going to put the object after you pick it up?
- How does the big claw open and close?
- What do you think is inside the claw?

Procedures

Review the procedures sections Christina and Freda designed in Figures 7.2, 7.4, and 7.6 as you read through these sections. In each of the three cycles, Christina and Freda inserted questions they had designed for their plan into their procedures, helping them to be prepared to ask questions as the implementation proceeded. Look at the many questions they developed for cycle 1 or cycle 2 (see Chapter 6) and then revisit the observation records for each cycle (see Chapter 4). You will see that Christina and Freda did not use all of their questions. Their observation records show little teacher intervention and a lot of conversation among the children. Developing these questions in the procedures section prepared the teachers' mindsets for facilitating the children's emerging inquiry.

Notice how Christina and Freda generated carefully thought-out procedures with a developmental progression for learning. They considered their meeting time as a guided mini-lesson for generating rich thinking and conversation among children. You can follow their example by asking questions like the following as you prepare your procedures section:

- Will children benefit if I provide a discussion of documentation from today before returning to an experience with the same materials tomorrow or in a few days?

- If we watch a video, will it help children to learn about a new material or concept prior to discussion?

Did You Think of How You Will Get Children Ready for the Experience?

In cycle 1 (see the procedures list in Fig. 7.2), during whole group class meeting time, children were reminded of the video they viewed, asked open-ended questions on what they remembered prior to revisiting the video, and then guided to discuss more about incinerators. Questions were designed to elicit children's thinking about what they knew and wanted to know so Christina and Freda could document their ideas for future planning.

In cycle 2 (see the procedures list in Fig. 7.4), the open-ended arrangement of materials that had been holding children's interest in their recent explorations was an invitation for children to enter the center and explore independently. The plans allowed for a flow of children to enter into and out of the planned center, allowing Christina and Freda to notice which children had a keen interest in exploring how to use these handheld claws.

In cycle 3 (see the procedures list in Fig. 7.6), the setup was provided in the context of a smaller group gathering at the kitchen table. It allowed Christina and Freda to work closely on the detailed dissembling processes with small core groups of children.

Did You Think of How You Will Introduce the Provocation Processes, Which Might Include Materials, Questions, Conversations, Modeling, Listing, or Diagramming?

In cycle 1 (see Fig. 7.2), the provocation was introduced in a small group setting, using a computer with a split screen: one for video viewing and discussion, the other for documenting children's questions and theories.

In cycle 2 (see Fig. 7.4), the materials were the overarching guide for the children's experiences with the handheld claws. The teachers observed, providing time for exploration before entering the play with intentional questions relevant to the children's actions. Christina and Freda considered that peer support would guide the experiences as peers explained and demonstrated their findings.

In cycle 3 (see Fig. 7.6), Christina and Freda planned some prediction questions to initiate the process of taking apart the intriguing tools (i.e., handheld claws). Intentional questions were prepared to guide the processes as needed, while allowing for children to manage as much of the process as they could on their own.

Did You Think of How You Will Plan for the Session with Children to Close?

In cycle 1 (see Fig. 7.2), the closing process involved Christina and Freda inviting children to share their thinking about incinerators with a partner and then as a group.

In cycle 2 (see Fig. 7.4), the closing discussion elicited the investigators' ideas about their new knowledge of the opening and closing mechanisms of the claws, and the documentation of their conversation was referenced as tool for revisiting together in the future.

In cycle 3 (see Fig. 7.6), the closing discussion elicited the children's ideas about the ways the handheld claws might be like the claws in the incinerator they saw in the video.

Did You Describe How You Will Document the Children's Play?

For each of the three COI cycles, the teachers mentioned that documentation would be in the form of video, pictures, and anecdotal notes. They could have also noted in cycle 1 that they would be recording ideas for exploration in a K-W-L chart on the computer. Children's drawings, diagrams, or other forms of work can also be noted as forms of documenting their experiences.

Implementing Your Inquiry Provocation

You've designed an inquiry provocation plan and you are excited to set up and implement this with children. First, take time to revisit your plan to be sure that you know all the details. Become familiar with the materials, being clear on the setup and the questions you will have ready to pose, and decide which types of documentation will be best to capture the children's engagement (e.g., observation records and photos or video, children's artifacts, easel charts).

Set Up and Facilitate Play

Teachers facilitate in ways that allow children to do more and teachers to do less. They use observation records and photos or video to capture observations of the setup (provocation) and the children engaged in play.

Get to Know the Materials

Think about whether you are familiar with the materials you have included in your plan. You can experiment with and explore the materials yourself or with other teachers ahead of time. We recommend that teachers include a materials exploration in their staff meeting at least once monthly to help everyone gain fluency with the properties of the materials and consider the kinds of thinking each material might support.

Consider how complex the materials are. What kinds of thinking and questions surface as you explore the materials? Will they be hard for children to manipulate without adult intervention? Will the materials challenge children in ways that they can problem solve, be creative, extend their thinking about the topic of focus, and stretch them a bit but still allow them to work independently? Do the materials have the ability to capture your own interest for a long time, and will they keep the children's attention?

From your experimentation, you can learn about the ways the materials might lead children's thinking in relation to your plan. This sort of exploration will help you to be better prepared to facilitate children's interactions with the materials.

Set Up the Environment Before Inviting Children

As noted in Chapter 6, you will be thinking very specifically about how you will set up the materials in an inquiry provocation center. It is also important to be sure that your provocation is prepared in that center prior to children entering the classroom. This enables you to be available to observe and facilitate with children. As your emergent inquiry project progresses over time, you may have inquiry provocation plans for more than one provocation center. Therefore, you will want to have each ready before children come into the classroom. As you may recall from Chapter 2, you can invite children to share what they noticed that is new in the classroom during an informal classroom meeting at the start of the day. This can be a great motivator for children to want to explore with new materials you may have added to an ongoing provocation.

Use of Your Planned Questions with Children

You have prepared several questions or prompt statements to use with children in relation to this provocation. It may not be necessary to use any or all of these questions, as the materials and interactions among the children might guide their thinking in ways that support the inquiry you're planning around. Through the process of designing questions for the provocation, you will feel better equipped to frame relevant questions that emerge during play that you had not considered during planning.

Participation in Play

As we've stated many times in previous sections, plan so that children do more and you do less. Allow yourself to hold back and observe carefully to allow for children's autonomy during the exploration or play experience, entering when you notice that there is a need for support. In this way, your interactions with the children are akin to responsive conversations in which children drive the flow of the interaction.

Documenting the Implementation

When you have prepared to implement your inquiry provocation plan by following the recommendations just provided, you will find that you have more time to hold back to observe and document the play. This is an important feature of this process, as this documentation on the COI Observation Record form and with photos or video will accumulate and become part of the focus of your next cycle.

Length of Provocation

Some of your inquiry provocation plans will be designed for a focused small core group discussion and some for a focused classroom meeting with the whole class. These may last for a long or short session, depending on children's needs to communicate their ideas.

Provocations can be designed to remain in a center for many days. Sometimes children may not work in depth with the materials right away. They may require more time to become familiar with the materials in order to relate them to the concepts that engage them within the inquiry project. At other times, children will be able to quickly grasp the relationships between the materials and the concepts of the inquiry project. Either way, it is important to leave your provocation out in a center for many days so the children have the opportunity to enter and leave, perhaps spending a lot of time there one day and time in another center another day, knowing that they can come back to this focus. Thinking related to the inquiry project often surfaces in the minds of participants when they take a break from the materials. These new ideas and insights then guide the participants to return to the inquiry provocation center to experiment further.

In addition, leaving your inquiry provocation in the center for a length of time will allow children outside the small core group to enter into the center periodically, which can bring new perspectives to the inquiry project. Allowing time also means that you can observe and collect many observation records for developing your next cycle.

For Further Reflection and Inquiry

The COI Inquiry Provocation Plan form is where you solidify your approach for your next emergent inquiry experience. You are pulling information and ideas from the many forms on which you have already documented your thinking about what children know and wonder, as well as questions and materials that can guide their inquiry. The process of reflecting several times, from observing to interpreting to developing action questions and provocations, deepens your mindset for connecting children's possible intentions to the plans you design. Knowing that your reflective practices have guided you to design a well-thought-out plan, you can strengthen your ability to facilitate a next inquiry provocation session in which you will be closely connected to the goals of the materials and questions you've organized. This allows you to observe and enjoy the discovery and learning processes that will likely reach beyond your expectations. Following the implementation of your inquiry provocation plan, you will want to reflect on the ways the implementation with children met the goals of your plan and the ways learning standards were addressed. This reflection will be documented in the COI Reflective Evaluation form discussed in the next chapter.

For deeper reflection on planning and implementing provocations in your classroom, try these suggestions:

1. Gather the planning documents you have been using prior to reading this chapter to review and compare.

   a. What do you notice?

   b. Did you allow for children to be independent explorers, to engage in long and rich conversations with little teacher input, and to form their own questions and solve their own problems?

2. Think back on experiences with children in the last month and note your thoughts on the ways you have been a director instead of a facilitator, asking questions like the following:

   a. Were you using directives? If so, what was the intention of each directive?

   b. Did you have a specific, one-directional outcome you expected?

   c. Were you able to allow children autonomy to explore materials on their own so you could enter their experiences minimally with questions or statements?

   d. Were you thoughtful about when to enter or withhold from entering into children's experiences?

3. Thinking back on an experience or ahead to your plans, have you allocated enough time to satisfy children's needs for digging into an exploration to discover problems and questions and pursue possible solutions? Have you supported, or will you support, children to move from more simple play to more complex play?

4. Reflect back or, as you go through your week, think about how well you have prepared the learning environments in your classroom. Have you set up centers where the materials clearly invite long-term engagement through the day? Do the children know what to do when entering a learning center, or do they need a lot of teacher direction?

CHAPTER 8
Developing Reflective Evaluation

You improve your teaching by reflecting on your experiences and those of the children in your classroom (Castle 2012). Each form of the COI system promotes teacher reflection. The thinking processes associated with each form build on reflective thinking documented in the previous forms, helping you revisit your practices as a planner, facilitator, co-learner, and evaluator of learning. Reflection goes beyond descriptions of experience and becomes meaningful when it leads to clear goals for the areas of your practice where you want to develop more focused awareness (Edwards, Gandini & Forman 2012; Stacey 2009, 2011; Wien 2008).

The deeper reflection practices prompted by the COI Reflective Evaluation form (see Appendix 5) include taking a closer look at the ways children respond to your inquiry provocations and their peers, the ways you interact with children to question and facilitate learning, and what you notice about the ways your design of the provocation environment and materials have guided the children's inquiry.

Your job is to promote children's various ideas about what they are doing and noticing within the classroom so they are able to construct their theories about the subject of their play. While implementing your planned emergent inquiry session, you pay close attention to clues to the children's thinking processes. Each child sees the world differently. As an emergent inquiry teacher, you should be highly aware of how each child sees objects, people, and experiences and keep in mind how children interpret and understand the world around them. In the first two sections of the COI Reflective Evaluation form, you can look back on observation records, along with photos or video, to consider what the children's reactions reveal about what they are thinking and learning. A third section guides you to consider from different viewpoints, yours and the children's, what was or was not successful about a particular exploration session.

Facilitating play in ways that allow children more authority in their processes can be difficult in the beginning. It is challenging to hold back, observe, not step in too early, or tell the children what to do. It is critical for you to understand what it means to promote children's thinking, to know when to allow children the autonomy to take their play as far as they can without assistance. You will learn a lot about your facilitation skills while facilitating your inquiry implementation plan and afterward, during a reflection process responding to prompts on the COI Reflective Evaluation form.

As you gain more experience using emergent inquiry curriculum, you will learn to set up the environment in ways that invite children to join the planned play but also guide them to discover certain ideas that you think will extend and deepen their inquiry. Think back to the bluegrass music study (Chapter 3), particularly the ways that the teacher-designed stage invited children to perform and how the responsive provocation of the music writing center inspired children to write music they could read and play. On the COI Reflective Evaluation form, you will review the ways the learning environment influenced the children's thinking and exploration. You will consider the ways the specific area of the room, the intentional materials, and the materials setup guided the experience.

In addition, the COI Reflective Evaluation form asks you to determine which early learning standards have been met or addressed as a follow-up to the implementation. Assessing for standards after observations of your planned inquiry is an important feature of this system and is very different from many early childhood assessment methods, which begin their planning processes around specific standards. Beginning with standards may lead to short or isolated activities where the possibilities for children to connect their theories across learning experiences can be limited (Fuchs & Deno 1991).

Getting to Know the COI Reflective Evaluation Record Form

The COI Reflective Evaluation form is used to look back on the setup of the provocation center and your implementation of the inquiry provocation plan to consider children's reactions, your facilitation, learning outcomes, what went well, what was unexpected, what you perceive that didn't go well, and how to build on the inquiry. This is also where you can check on the standards that were met during the exploration. Through long-term emergent inquiry processes, children will most likely meet many more standards than you anticipate.

By planning emergent inquiry curricula around children's thinking and conceptual development, you are meeting the children at their interest level and skill level, where learning is challenging but achievable. This will engage children in learning processes over longer periods of time, and the day-to-day experiences you design will naturally link together in the children's minds. Then you can call on your expert knowledge of standards to reflect back on the learning that occurred, using standards as a checklist to make visible the many that were addressed and to note any that were not part of the inquiry process. With this information, you can design plans for incorporating the unmet standards in ways that stay close to the thinking and purposes of children within the framework of the ongoing inquiry.

Identifier Information

The identifier information you will record on the COI Reflective Evaluation form includes the Big Idea or thread of inquiry that is the focus of the experiences you are evaluating as a tag, the names of the interpreters, the children involved in the exploration, and the time, date, and area of the classroom.

Children's Reaction

Do you have evidence that the children were engaged? Think about and describe what the experience was like for the children in ways that describe their goals and strategies for meeting those goals. What was the social atmosphere?

If you think children were engaged in the experience you just facilitated, this is where you provide the evidence to support your claim. For example, a statement that "Children explored the clay" is less clear than a statement saying, "Children manipulated the clay with their hands, their fists, their elbows, and their fingers, trying many methods for the duration of the constructive play time."

The social atmosphere refers to the ways children engage in the context of others. This is where you comment on children's choices to work alone or with peers and the effects of these choices on the children's experiences. For example, children may be cooperating with peers in ways that move the processes forward. A lack of cooperation might lead you to consider the ways the environment and materials are affecting the interactions and what adjustments might support cooperation in the future. Noting the benefits or challenges of working alone or in groups better prepares you to support both individual and group processes.

Learning

Do you have evidence that the children learned? Citing evidence from your observation to pinpoint what you think children learned from a session takes some experience and effort. Stating what happened during a learning experience is different from stating the learning you observed. You should be able to answer the question "What did the children learn and how do you know that they learned it?" Sentence templates could be helpful: "We know that they _____ when they said _____" or "The children's [actions, statements] showed us that they were _____."
Here is an example from a toddler classroom:

The children used the flashlights outside and inside the box that was covered with black cloth. We knew that they recognized that the box was dark when they said "Dark" and "Black" on entering or leaving the box. We knew they were learning that the flashlight makes darker spaces light when they intentionally sought out dark corners of the classroom to use the flashlight, showing the same delight as when they used the flashlight to light up the inside of the cardboard box. The quizzical expressions we noticed when they turned the flashlight off and on in the brighter sections of the room showed us that they were testing the results of their actions and that they might have some questions about the relationship of the light they project into a lighted area.

How Did the Session Match Your Intentions?

Think about and describe in detail what the experience was like for you and how the experience aligned with the rationale you presented in your inquiry provocation plan. You will write the ways your intentions aligned with those you designed to extend children's thinking in your inquiry provocation plan. Think back on the intentions of children in the experience you just facilitated. State in this section how *their* intentions matched those in your plan.

In the example with the box and light exploration, the teachers were satisfied that the children not only explored the darkness of the box but that they went

beyond the teachers' expectations, extending their explorations of the flashlight in relation to other dark areas of the classroom. The children had initially been noticing light and shadows in the classroom, and the provocation with the box gave them opportunities to explore related concepts with new materials.

What Did You Learn About Facilitating Play?

Think about the influence of the materials and setup, your interactions, and your guiding questions or provocation statements on the children. Write about the ways these interventions affected the children's experiences. Did they motivate, support, stifle, or extend thinking? Did you find that you didn't need to intervene with words because you observed children independently following their own interesting pursuits within the context of your provocation?

You may find, as many teachers do, that over time you learn to step back and provide more freedom for children to explore materials and direct their own play. Children engage in unexpected and thoughtful ways when given time to explore without interference. A session may not go well because the plan is too teacher directed. Rather than attract children to the experience, too much teacher intervention may bore the children to the extent that they leave the area to choose another place to play.

In the example with the cardboard box and the flashlights, the teachers stated that they were worried the children were losing interest in the experience when they moved away from being in the box to using the flashlights in the classroom. But the teachers realized that the children remained interested in the box as they kept returning to it after exploring other light and dark areas of the classroom, comparing the effects of the flashlight in a variety of locations. This required little interaction from the teachers beyond proximity to document, which did seem to support the children in knowing that the teachers were interested in what they were doing. The teachers also narrated the children's actions, such as "I see you are shining the flashlight into that dark shelf, and it gets lighter" (Curtis 2017). Providing language for what children were experiencing seemed to be helpful; the children began to use words like *light, dark, darker, very dark,* and *very light* as they explored with the flashlights.

What Next?

How will you build on this learning? In what ways can you provide differentiated support to encourage diverse learners to participate in the inquiry? As you reflect on ways to build on the children's learning within the context of the Big Idea of the plan you just implemented with children, document your thoughts in the "What Next?" section of the COI Reflective Evaluation form.

Teachers are typically refreshed and energized after a successful experience with children, so much so that many ideas for extensions bubble through their minds. This section is the perfect place for you to note these initial thoughts down to use as a framework for planning and interpreting at a later time when you revisit the observation data to more deeply interpret this play.

In addition to writing about ways to build on the learning you observed among the children, write some ways you might build on what you learned about facilitating the children's play. For example, comment on your ability to enter the play or to use questions effectively. Note ideas about materials that can frame concepts in new ways. After the cardboard box and flashlight study, teachers reflected that at some point they could introduce colored flashlight bulbs or use cellophane paper on windows in the box to add a new dimension to the projection of light and formation of shadows. These teachers were connecting their next step ideas to their Big Idea regarding the exploration of light in relation to shadows.

Standards Checklist

What curricular standards were met during this session? Be sure to review all of the curriculum and state standards your program is responsible for addressing in relation to the play you observed. Over and over again, teachers comment on how they are meeting so many standards in many discipline areas within one emergent inquiry exploration. Be thorough in this section, stating all the standards demonstrated by the children. Then you can clearly identify which standards you might not have addressed so that you can design ways for incorporating them into the next phases of the children's inquiry.

By listing evidence with each standard, you can easily organize assessments for individual children in the context of the emergent inquiry project work with peers. Here are three examples among the many standards teachers noted with related evidence from the light and shadow project. The teachers cited the Tennessee Early Learning Development Standards (TN-ELDS) for toddlers:

- Approaches to Learning / Engages and Interacts: AL.37–48.3 Demonstrate awareness of connection between prior and new knowledge.

  › While holding their flashlights Cory, Kai, and Amelie all run out of the dark box, pointing the light onto the surfaces of wall, over the surfaces of toys in various centers, out the windows and back into the box. They are relating the information about the way the flashlight works outside back to their experiences with the light inside the box.

- Approaches to Learning / Flexibility and Inventiveness: AL.37–48.5 Continue to ask questions for information or clarification.

  › Their experimentation with the flashlight reveals that these toddlers, Cory, Kai, and Amelie, are using actions to ask questions about the light in relation to different environmental settings.

- Math, Measurement and Data: MA.37–48.5 Become aware of his body and personal space during active exploration of physical environment.

  › Cory, Kai, and Amelie have an awareness of their personal space as they move easily from center to center, out of and back into the box, directly aiming the flashlight onto specific surfaces and spaces in the classroom and out the window.

Documentation

How effective was your choice of documentation for this session? Note your thoughts on other methods to use that would be more helpful for your needs. Develop a plan, as needed, to improve your own skill with documentation. In this section you are noting the success or needed improvement for your documentation of children.

As we will explore in depth in Chapter 9, documentation is a complex process. Teachers collect observation records, children's artifacts (e.g., drawings, photos of structures or sculptures), notes on children's dialogue, video, photos of sequential processes, and other such items to gather evidence of learning. Often teachers exclaim that they wish they had not let a child take home that drawing that represented rich thinking related to a project, or they wish they had been better prepared to capture learning moments. Consider when it will be valuable to use photographs to document children's processes with materials. It is helpful to take a clear snapshot of each drawing from an exploration just in case a drawing is lost, ripped, or transformed in a later session as a child reworks the drawing. Having a visual record of each phase is useful for discussions with the children about their thinking at each phase of the process. This applies to any ongoing project work where the product might transform from one day to another or every few minutes.

You will also want to think about when it would be helpful to record children's statements during a conversation and whether you want to use a chart so the documentation is visible to the children. Think about whether video or photographs would be the best way to represent the processes you are planning for children.

These are the kinds of questions to reflect on at the end of a session as you consider the many options for documentation in the next session. Reflecting on the success and needed improvements of your documentation prepares you for future success.

Using the COI Reflective Evaluation Form
Learning from the Incinerator Project

Three cycles of Christina and Freda's COI Reflective Evaluation form from the incinerator project are shared for you to review and learn how to use this form (Figs. 8.1 and 8.2). The comments in this section refer to their reflective evaluation of cycle 3 in relation to criteria for successful use of this form that are noted in the COI Reflective Evaluation Checklist (see Appendix 5).

REVISIT THE SESSION AND EVALUATE IT AS A LEARNING EXPERIENCE
Emergent curricula give children learning experiences and opportunities to develop their
competencies, their theories, and their sense of mastery over knowledge, circumstances, and skills.
Reflect on this session and evaluate its worth for both the children and the teachers.
AREA: Big carpet
PARTICIPANTS: Open so children can explore according to interest and choice
DATE & TIME: 2/3 during P.M. investigations

CHILDREN'S REACTION: Do you have evidence that the children were engaged? Think about and
describe what the experience was like for the children in ways that describe their goals and their strategies
for meeting those goals. Were children cooperative? Did they experience collaboration?

When I introduced the hand-held claw/grabbers to the children during group time, I mentioned that they would
get to explore the claws as an investigation for the afternoon. The children seemed very eager to want to explore
the activity, since I heard, "I want to do that!" "That looks cool!" "Can I do the claw first?" I chose four children to
explore the activity first, and then from there, I timed them and had them give their grabber to another child. I
observed how the children explored with the claws/grabbers, and I noticed how they focused on the lever part
of the claw and getting used to picking up the recycled materials. The children also made connections with the
garbage incinerator video. For example, Muse said, "I saw this in the garbage video." Some children were also
making observations about the claws, which told me they were engaged and excited. For example, J.D. pointed to
the actual claw part and said, "This is the claw's mouth." On their own, the children made piles of garbage and
piles that needed to turn into ash, which told me they were also making connections from the video. Overall, the
atmosphere was very calm, and the children were focused on the claws and investigating how they worked.

LEARNING: Do you have evidence that the children learned?

During the activity, when asked how the claws worked, Hassan said, "When you push down, it opens and then
closes." Matthew said, "When you push here, it closes." When asked how the lever closes it, he replied, "This metal
thing. It goes through it. Then, it closes." This told me that they were making sense of cause and effect, which was
one of the main objectives for this activity. The children were also able to make connections with the big claw from
the video. For example, when asked how the little claws are like the big claw, Muse said, "It can grab stuff." Renato
replied, "It looks bigger and better. It can pick up more things. These are just pretend claws." Fatme replied, "These
claws are smaller. You can pinch." All of these responses told me that they were making associations with the
garbage incinerator video and the claws they were exploring. While James picked up the materials, he said, "We
need to take them to the roaster." This showed me that he was also making a connection because he was most
likely talking about the combustion chamber where the fire is. When Ian explored the claws and was asked how
the claw worked, he replied, "You just have to pull it back. It controls it, and you can grab stuff." Ian used different
types of vocabulary terms to describe the process, which showed me he was learning through his explorations.
Overall, I believe the children achieved the objectives intended for the lesson and learned through the activity.

HOW DID THE SESSION MATCH YOUR INTENTIONS? Think about the interactions
and development of the children; think about the teachers.
Prior to the lesson, I expected the children to explore with the claws and create a mini incinerator by designating
areas. This did happen among the children, since they created a trash pile, feed hopper, and then a pile of garbage
that they pretended was already turned into ash. For example, J.D. pointed to the pile of recycled materials and said,
"That's the garbage. We have to put it in the feed hopper." When the children were putting the materials in the feed
hopper, I overheard Renato saying to the other children, "Stay away from this. It's the feed hopper. It's dangerous.
There is fire at the bottom." That showed me that he was making connections and understood the process of each of
the parts. I also expected the children to pick up as much of the materials as they could with the claws, which they
did, and they also focused on how the claw moved while pushing on the lever.

Figure 8.1. First page of the COI Reflective Evaluation form for cycle 3 of the incinerator project.

WHAT DID YOU LEARN ABOUT FACILITATING PLAY? Think about the influence of the materials and setup on the children and about the influence of your questions or provocation statements.

Providing claws along with the trash engaged the children successfully. It allowed them to go beyond just moving the claws. I noticed Hassan and Muse passing materials to each other from one claw to another without letting it touch the ground, which I didn't anticipate any of the children to do. Questions focusing children to think about how the claws work guided in-depth exploration, which led to inventions resembling the children's notion of a conveyor belt. This also showed me that they were able to incorporate collaboration into the activity, which was an overall goal in relation to our Big Idea.

WHAT NEXT? How will you build on this learning? In what ways can you provide differentiated support for diverse learners?

Since the children were so interested in how the claw worked, as well as the cause and effect aspect of the process, we are going to investigate the inside of the claw next week. This will involve taking apart the claws using tools, but we won't show the tools to the children right away. We will ask them questions of how they think we can open the claws and see what is inside. We want them to focus on investigating how it works on their own. This will allow the children to gain a better understanding of cause and effect, especially when it comes to the inside of the claw and how it works.

STANDARDS CHECKLIST: What curricular standards were met during this session?

ELE: Approaches to Learning

Early Learning Expectation: Creativity-Imagination-Visualization. Children demonstrate a growing ability to use originality or vision when approaching learning; use imagination, show ability to visualize a solution or new concept.

Emerging Indicators:

- Make connections with situations or events, people or stories.
- Create new images or express ideas. Relates to 2nd and 3rd bullets
  - (Pulled lever up and down) It helps the claw open and close. (Pointing to the claw.) This is the claw's mouth, and he's eating everything.
- Expand current knowledge onto a new solution, new thinking or new concept.
- Grow in eagerness to learn about and discuss a growing range of topics, ideas, and tasks. Relates to 3rd and 4th bullets
  - It's too fat! (Picking up the tube)
  - When you push down, it opens and closes.
  - The smaller claw opens easier.

Early Learning Expectation: Initiative-Engagement-Persistence-Attentiveness. Children demonstrate the quality of showing interest in learning; pursue learning independently.

Emerging Indicators:

- Initiate "shared thinking" with peers and adults.
- Show growing capacity to maintain concentration in spite of distractions and interruptions.
- Explore, experiment, and ask questions freely.
  - Throughout the conversation you can see children initiating on their own as well as responding to teachers' prompts, but also they inspire teachers' thinking and questioning, like with this teacher question, "But it's so far away. How can it close it?"

Many other emerging indicators were noted that are not represented here due to space.

DOCUMENTATION. How effective was your choice of documentation for this session? Note your thoughts on other methods to use that would be more helpful for your needs. Develop a plan, as needed, to improve your own skill with documentation.

This session was documented through photos and anecdotal notes. The photos helped us recall a lot of details and helped us illustrate what we documented in our written records.

Figure 8.2. Second page of the COI Reflective Evaluation form for cycle 3 of the incinerator project.

Evaluate Learning

The teachers noted specific comments children made and how these showed what they were learning from the experience.

Does Your Description of the Children's Reactions Provide Enough Detail for the Reader to Visualize Children's Strategies and Thinking in the Context of a Particular Learning Environment?

The teachers reflected on the children's reactions during the exploration and consider the questions about this that appear on the form.

Christina and Freda noted that the children's goals and strategies focused on the lever part of the claw and how the handheld claw worked. They also noticed the connections the children made to the garbage incinerator video they observed in an earlier session. An example of children's comments about the video content was provided as evidence of engagement and of children relating this experience to a prior experience. The teachers' detailed description of the activity and examples painted a clear picture of children's goals and thinking. They expressed children's intense focus and calm manners as representation of positive emotions during play.

Did You Describe What the Activity Was Like for the Children with Enough Detail that the Reader Can Clearly Visualize and Understand the Events from Your Perspective?

Christina and Freda described how the children created their own play agenda, including the passing of materials to each other from one claw to another without letting it touch the ground. Many children were inspired to follow this goal of the play, which led to a new goal of passing the materials into a pretend incinerator. One child would pick up the garbage with the claw and pass it to another child with a claw, who would put the garbage in the feed hopper. Christina and Freda said the children shared and listened to the ideas of others, encouraged others to join in play,

and commented on other children's ideas, which demonstrated a cooperative atmosphere. Their plan allowed for children to creatively work together.

When You State that Learning Has Occurred, Do Your Examples Provide Evidence from Specific Observed Interactions that Led to the Knowledge Construction?

Christina and Freda tightly linked ideas about the learning to examples. Statements about the workings of the claw and making sense of the cause and effect of its actions were followed by quotes from children that highlighted their developing understanding. Christina and Freda noted how the children made a connection between the ways the handheld claws worked and their ideas about the workings of the mechanical claws they observed in the video in a previous session. They associated children's understanding with their statements.

Does the Learning You Note Relate to Your Action Question from the COI Inquiry Provocation Plan?

In their inquiry provocation plan, Christina and Freda's action question was "What are the parts/process of the incinerator?" This question encompassed the incinerator as a whole as well just one part of it—how the claw worked. These teachers identified a lot of conversation among children about the way the handheld claws worked and their thinking about their function in relation to the claws they observed in the video. This evidence of relating thinking about experience and function in present and past situations showed development in children's thinking.

Did You List Relevant Learning Standards from *All* Domains of Learning for Your State and Age Group?

The teachers cited four learning expectations and their related emerging indicators as references of the learning they observed. The four early learning expectations they noted focus on creativity (imagination, visualization), initiative (engagement, persistence, attentiveness), curiosity (inquiry, question), and reasoning (problem solving). These standards matched the learning that occurred during the session and were listed with evidence from the play session.

Did You Write a Statement For Each Standard You Noted that Shows the Way It Connects to the Learning Outcomes from this Play Session?

State standards for early childhood programs are typically listed numerically such that each number aligns with a statement describing the component of the standard as an easily observable indicator. It is important for teachers to be very familiar with the standards they are expected to use and articulate each as a complete sentence or statement so others will be clear on the relationship of the standard to the experiences that are documented in all the COI forms for each cycle. The teachers who facilitated the incinerator project wrote out the standards as statements on the COI Reflective Evaluation form.

Evaluate Implementation and Documentation

As a reflective teacher, you will return to your documentation to assess how useful it has been for supporting your understanding of children and for planning. The items in this section ask you to critically reflect on your documentation quality and technique.

Did You Describe Ways the Session Matched or Didn't Match Your Expectations with Enough Detail that the Reader Can Clearly Visualize and Understand the Events from Your Perspective?

Christina and Freda explained children's expectations and unexpected positive learning outcomes, such as peer collaboration. Initially, they expected children to explore with the claws and create a mini incinerator. The children not only explored the intended ideas but also generated several new ideas, like acting out the recycling process, creating a trash pile and feed hopper, and pretending to turn a pile of garbage into ash.

The teachers also explained how the children were inventive in incorporating peers into their play: "We have to put it in the feed hopper." Use of the term *we* reveals children's view of themselves as a part of community of learners.

Did You Describe the Ways the Materials and Setup Influenced the Children's Thinking and Learning?

Christina and Freda responded to the materials at length. They indicated that they learned a lot from the children and that they were able to be open to the children using the materials in unexpected ways, such as when the children formulated a cooperative game using the claws to pass materials back and forth. The influence of the incinerator video on the children's simulation of the claw's movement was also recorded as significant by these teachers. Choosing materials to guide thinking and enable children to explore in open-ended ways allowed children's thinking to emerge beyond Christina and Freda's expectations.

Did You Describe the Ways Your Facilitation Strategies Were Successful or Need Improvement?

Christina and Freda mentioned their facilitation in several areas of the COI Reflective Evaluation form. For example, in the section on learning, they noted that they intentionally chose four children to explore the play first and allowed each to focus on their own goals and strategies to make sense of the provocation. They mostly focused on the ways the intentionally chosen materials guided the thinking during play.

While it is possible that they reflected on their own questioning in the process of documenting their thoughts in other sections of the COI Reflective Evaluation form, using this section to make their thinking visible regarding their questioning and interactions would be a first step toward making any necessary improvements.

Projecting Next Steps Forward in the Curriculum

The COI process leads you to a state of mind where you are continually reflecting on experiences as a means of guiding learning forward, which is the emphasis of this next section.

Did You Reflect on the Children's Current Goals and Ideas and Describe the Best Possible Next Learning Step in Detail?

Christina and Freda analyzed the children's emerging curiosity about the way a claw works and planned for investigating the inside of the claw. They were thinking with a developmental perspective about how children learn by planning to allow children to build theories about and goals for learning about the mechanics of the claws before providing tools to open the claws and see the inside. Rather than focus on rote skills such as identifying names and parts of the claw, the teachers focused on high-level thinking skills and related learning back to the Big Idea.

For Further Reflection and Inquiry

The COI Reflective Evaluation form guides you through the meta-reflective processes of a structured reflection, assisting you in becoming a more competent teacher. The goal for structured reflection is to reflect on (1) what it means to learn and (2) what it means to teach based on what is known about learning (Brooks 2011).

Emergent curriculum involves risk. The provocations you design have the potential to work really well; they may likely guide children in unexpected directions you hadn't thought of. The COI Reflective Evaluation form is a helpful tool for understanding *why* the play

followed a certain unanticipated path, the learning that emerged for you and children, and the alignment of these experiences with your inquiry provocation plan, your facilitation, and your documentation. As you practice revisiting your planned provocations, you will gain confidence with planning and implementing ongoing COI cycles that extend into long-term projects. The next chapter introduces you to documentation panels, a process for synthesizing the learning within long periods of your inquiry process in order to share with families, children, and your school community.

For deeper reflection on developing and using reflective evaluation processes in your classroom, try these suggestions:

1. Select *one* section of the COI Reflective Evaluation form and think back on experiences from your classroom in recent days. For example, consider the ways materials in a learning center guided children's thinking.

    a. What important details do you note about the materials? About the learning? Are they related?

    b. Do you find it difficult to accurately reflect? Might better documentation help you?

    c. Think about what you will do to document the influence of materials on play the next time children are in the classroom, and write it down.

    d. Follow up by reviewing how your documentation shows the influence of materials on play, and compare this reflection to your first.

    e. Share and discuss with your teaching team or director.

2. Repeat the process above with each section of the COI Reflective Evaluation form.

CHAPTER 9
Creating Documentation Panels

Documentation refers to the many ways you record learning experiences within your emergent inquiry process. You will collect many observation records; COI planning forms; children's artifacts such as drawings or photos of products; notes on children's dialogue, videos, photos of sequential processes; and more as part of your ongoing documentation process. Many of these forms of documentation can be posted in provocation centers to reflect the learning taking place and to inspire children to revisit their previous experiences, which triggers their minds to recall the related thinking and learning. This chapter discusses documentation panels (see Fig. 9.1), which tell the stories of the progression of learning over a period of time, making thinking and learning visible.

To create a documentation panel, you will synthesize the many forms of documentation you have collected through your emergent inquiry process to communicate the learning that occurred. Children see themselves in documentation panels and reflect back on what they've done and learned. Documentation panels articulate the learning in meaningful ways that invites teachers, family members, and the school and larger community into conversations about the interpretations of learning and designs for curricular extensions, helping them to better understand how children learn. To effectively tell the learning story you must go beyond what the children learned to include information that also makes visible your teaching methods and practices. Let readers know the interpretations and questions that guided your planning and facilitation throughout an emergent inquiry process (Hong 1998; Wien 2008; Wien, Guyevskey, & Berdoussis 2011).

A good documentation panel can walk a person through a project so that person understands the thought processes of both children and teachers. It communicates what the children were thinking, how and why the teachers provoked deeper

understanding, and what was ultimately learned by all. It reads like a good story, with a beginning, a middle, and an end.

Documentation panels are collections of data and may include

- Photographs

- Video

- Written observation records

- Text illuminating teachers' analysis and theories about children's learning and thinking

- Children's creations

- Representations of teacher provocations

As you create these panels, you are carefully reflecting on the many elements of the learning to gain insights about the threads of inquiry and Big Ideas and to inspire new provocations for extending the inquiry (Hong & Forman 2000).

When you begin your journey with pedagogical documentation, you need to become comfortable with going public with your recounting of activities. Share your documentation panel first with a colleague to get feedback, and as you continue to create documentation panels you will gain confidence with the process. Strive to develop the technical and visual literacy skills required to arrange information graphically or digitally. *Visual literacy* refers to the organization of information on a page so that readers can follow the flow of a story in the way you, the author, intended. Pictures and text convey the events and related dialogue among children and teachers and any other participants. Including children's words and representations is critical to any good documentation panel to give insight into children's thought processes. Text in the form of teacher

A Professional Performance

Children were introduced to Bluegrass and Old-Time music with a performance from Lara Beth Poteat and David Rich, students from the Bluegrass, Old Time and Country Music Program at ETSU.

The musicians played songs from three eras of the genre that reflect stories and places in the region.

- Tennesse Waltz—children were inspired to learn the waltz when invited by teachers

- Gone, Gone—children say that Lara Beth's original song is jazzy, discriminating differences in the sounds and styles of songs from different eras. They also said the words "gone, gone, movin' like a freight train" represent a train like the one that moves by their school daily.

- Rocky Top—children recognize the words Tennessee in this song, and know this is where they live, their home. They also refer to the "Vols."

They asked musicians to play "This Land is Your Land," seeing the link in both songs as representing ideas about "home."

They also recognize Rocky Top as a mountain, like those in their region.

The children recognize the fiddle as a "violin." The student teacher, Ms. Rebecca has played this instrument many times in their class. They are now learning to refer to the violin as a "fiddle."

Catie: Fiddle in Bluegrass! (week four during a review of instrumental sounds and pictures)

Introduction to Bluegrass and Old Time Instruments

Children experience a hands on opportunity to hear, see and play the different instruments from the Bluegrass and Old Time Genres.

Early on they were recognizing the many instruments as guitars, most likely because they all have strings.

Jeremy and Catie show us that they know that you strum the strings to produce sounds.

Discriminating High and Low Sounds

Children initially thought that the lower sounding string would be on the bottom (physically lower) and the higher sounding string would be on top (physically higher).

By picking the strings on real instruments they found that the higher string is on the bottom and the lower string is on the top.

Pictures above:
Devlin is playing the highest sounding string on the guitar; Chloe plays the lowest sounding string on the fiddle; Chloe plays the highest sounding string on the fiddle.

Children's drawings of High and Low Guitar Strings

Chloe draws the strings of a guitar. She knows that the highest sounding string is on the bottom and is thin, and that the lowest string on the top is fatter.

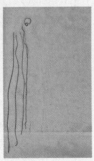

Left: Chloe shows an understanding that the high sound comes from the thin string (bottom). Carter G. (middle) and Catie (right) represent the strings of guitars as lines. They have carefully observed the guitar.

Figure 9.1. A section of a documentation panel from the beginning of the bluegrass study.

From Children's Interests to Children's Thinking

commentary shares your own reasoning as to what the actions or words of children reveal about what they may be thinking.

The core information necessary to construct a documentation panel is included in the COI system forms you fill out as part of your inquiries.

Documentation Panel Making as Continuous Professional Development

Numerous studies validate the concept of documentation as a key aspect of continuous teacher development (Edwards, Gandini, & Forman 2012; Giudici, Rinaldi, & Krechevsky 2001; Hong 1998). Teachers using the COI system to guide their observations, interpretations, and planning are able to reflect on their own teaching pedagogy in ways that help them recognize their strengths and weaknesses so they can continually improve their own practices around planning and facilitating learning with children. Many teachers begin their work with the COI having little understanding of children's theories and how to decide what to offer to support continuous inquiry. They develop skills in these areas as they document with the COI system (Broderick & Hong 2011). By the time you have accumulated data from several COI cycles, you will be ready to create a documentation panel because you will have the information you need to communicate your ideas about children's thinking and learning well organized within the COI documentation forms.

Components for Creating a Documentation Panel

A study one of us conducted (Hong 1998) outlines the content of a documentation panel that makes visible the thinking of children and teachers and informs the guidelines recommended here.

Teacher Commentary

This commentary illuminates the teachers' ideas of the purpose of the children's work in a storyline—a progression that clearly articulates what was learned and the concepts that the children addressed in the activity. For your teacher commentary, refer to your theories about the children's thinking and development on the COI Interpreting Thinking form (see Chapter 5) and COI Inquiry Provocation Plan form (see Chapter 7). Choose the theories related to the episodes you will represent in a documentation panel. This commentary should incorporate a background history of the project in descriptive text to set up an understanding for the sequence of learning. The background is information on the experiences of children that led to planning within your COI cycles. Teacher commentary also includes your detailed analysis (interpretive theories), to articulate the significance of each episode that is represented in the panel.

Include words that communicate your ideas and questions that arose while revisiting each phase of the learning process. Introduce the things you observed, what the children said or did that served as the guiding factors for the processes you are documenting. Discuss with your colleagues the learning processes you are trying to communicate, brainstorming words and using digital tools like Wordclouds or a thesaurus tool. The purpose of revisiting is to gain additional insight and to reconstruct the progression of the story of the children's learning so you can merge the earlier and current learning cohesively. Through this revisiting process, be open to developing new questions about the children's thinking that can further your inquiry with children, and include these as you tell your story. Inquiry is a research process. Typically, research leads to new questions. Include your new questions about possible new directions for the inquiry at the close of the panel.

Photographs of Children

Choose photographs from the COI Observation Record forms that show the progression of learning. Sequences are often needed to illustrate stages in a child's process—for example, three photos representing the child engaged in the early, middle, and final steps in a process of drawing, editing, and redrawing ideas about how an incinerator claw works. In these process-focused photo sequences, you are representing the children's engagement and thinking. Sometimes it is helpful to represent the product itself, with teacher commentary that interprets the meaning behind the work. Consider how to use the relationship and the sequence of the photographs to tell the story.

Think about the provocations you designed to guide the inquiry. Represent these in photographs with commentary that explains your rationale for choosing particular materials and your setup of the learning environment. Tell the reader if the process extended or challenged children with new materials and ideas or if it supported a revisiting process among children.

Children's Words and Actions

Present children's words as a working context of ideas, conversations where one child's thought rides on another child's thought, as opposed to a report on individual achievement. For example, in Figure 4.4 there is a section where three children are sharing ideas as they construct an incinerator with trash provided by teachers. Muse says, "We're going to make an incinerator. I want to make a grabber." Renato connects his comment to Muse's as he points to bottles and says, "These move to the fire." Then, pointing to a plastic container, Muse finalizes the idea with, "This can be the grabber. This is what it looks like," and he puts the bottle through the conveyor belt. In addition, the preservice teacher's comment from the memos column can be included in the panel with this dialogue to describe her understanding of the interaction: "Muse is able to recall the journey garbage takes through the incinerator."

Choose dialogue from the COI Observation Record form that reveals the children's theories about something, like how an object works. It is not necessary to include all that children say. Include dialogue that effectively tells the story and illustrates the complex thinking of the participants.

Editing the Panel

Ask yourself if the story you are communicating is clear to the reader. Ask peers to read your panel to see if there are any gaps in your story. Edit the panel to add any information, teacher commentary, photos, or dialogue that would provide clarity. Colleagues' feedback is a necessary step for completing your documentation panel.

Large-Format Documentation Panels from the Incinerator Project

Christine and Freda created two documentation panels on the incinerator project. One is shared in Figure 9.2. Take some time to review this panel, noticing the relationships of images to dialogue and how teachers' interpretive thinking and descriptions of processes relate to children's actions and words. Using a large-panel format (22" x 36") allowed the teachers to incorporate a lot of information.

The title of the documentation panel uses the words of children to represent the content being explored. This technique draws viewers to want to read more closely. Parents and families are interested in processes linked to children's words. You can see that subtitles are used to give more information about the processes as a lead-in to the background sections of each panel where the teachers discuss the play they have observed as a rationale for the provocations they are introducing. Descriptive text represents the actions of the children throughout. While minimal dialogue is included, the storytelling is clear.

While there are no captions with the images, each is aligned near text describing what the reader is viewing in the photograph. The words of the child whose drawing is represented in the panel are included in the drawing to help the reader interpret the child's thinking. It would be helpful to add a caption to the drawing with the child's name.

This panel has three sections. The background information below the title leads into the next section, and a third section provides thoughts on possible next directions for the inquiry. Photos are used to visually divide the sections and illustrate the learning.

"We're going to make an incinerator! It burns garbage down."

Representing garbage incinerators through building and drawing

Last semester the children began to show an interest in building. One afternoon, they worked together to build a castle with all the blocks in the block area when they realized their castle became a garbage incinerator. One of our children who had prior knowledge of incinerators sparked the interest of the other children who wanted to know more.

In order to extend the children's knowledge of garbage incinerators we all viewed a video on the process and journey garbage takes through the incinerator. The video showed what the parts of the incinerator are and what each part does.

Muse said, "Grabbers. They pick up garbage. The hard part is they have to use the controllers."

After the garbage goes through the feed hopper, the recycled materials are pulled out. Harry explained that, "It catches on fire," when the garbage travels through the combustion chamber on to the conveyor belt. The end product of the burned garbage was ash and electricity.

Building an incinerator

Part of our investigations for that day included building with recycled materials. The children worked together to gather materials from the big kitchen, brought this trash back, and began to build.

"We're going to make an incinerator!" exclaimed Muse.

The children lay connecting plastic bags on the floor and placed bottles and cans along this structure to simulate the conveyor belt.

Muse said, "Okay, it's on the hopper on the conveyor belt. Here is a pile of ash after it goes into the fire."

They transferred the materials to and from each part of their constructed incinerator. Once it reached the end Matthew said, "It turns into light!"

We extended their interest in building the incinerator by inviting them to draw individual plans that showed each part and the path the garbage takes. In the picture at left, Renato is referring to his drawing as he constructs it with Citiblocs and bricks. He said, "I made a claw. It grabs from the truck."

Next Steps

To gain insight into their main focus regarding incinerators we revisited the initial video in small groups and invited the children to think of ideas they wanted to investigate further. All the children had a specific interest in the claw/grabber. They wanted to know how it worked. Our next step is to investigate this idea with the children by exploring handheld grabbers and making connections to how they work like the grabber/claw of the incinerator.

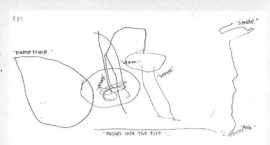

Figure 9.2. Documentation panel from the incinerator project.

Some teachers use PowerPoint for large-format panels because it is easiest to read on all computers. There may be other formats to choose from, such as Google Sheets, Adobe InDesign, and Publisher, but be sure that your readers and printer are compatible.

To create a large-format panel in PowerPoint, you can edit the dimensions in the Page Setup section of the program by going to File, then to Page Setup. You can save your final documentation panel as a PDF, a widely readable format that is not easy to edit if you are sharing with families, staff, and educators in your community. You will need a large-format printer to print panels larger than your desktop printer. Some desktop printers do include legal size paper (8″ × 14″), and some include pamphlet-size paper (11″ × 14″).

Your school may not have a large-format printer, in which case you can use 8.5″ × 11″ documents to create a documentation panel with a series of pages. These smaller panels can also be easily shared electronically with families via email or secure online accounts. Alternatively, you can print your documents and cut and paste photos and word content onto poster boards to create a larger panel.

Locating the Information on the COI Forms to Include the Panels

The panel in Figure 9.2 demonstrates the ease with which Christina and Freda were able to revisit and pull data from their COI forms to create their documentation panel. The children's words and photos can be traced back to the first cycle. The descriptive text and commentary were formulated by revisiting their COI Interpreting Thinking and Reflective Evaluation forms for each cycle. Photos that accompany each COI Observation Record form are also included in the documentation panel.

Small-Format Documentation Panel from a Classroom of 3- to 4-Year-Olds
Think White Project

This section presents parts of a small-format documentation panel that Deb, a preschool teacher, created using PowerPoint. Only one of the many slides in her documentation panel is included here (see Fig. 9.3). Deb's panel shares the experiences of a teacher-initiated provocation she designed that was inspired by a professional development exploration with materials where she was a participant.

In a program for early childhood teachers who work with emergent curriculum, Deb engaged in a materials exploration where her task was to respond to the prompt "Think white," using a variety of white papers in a range of sizes, thicknesses, and textures; a brush; a small amount of glue; 18-gauge wire; and scissors (Broderick & Hong 2005). She was asked to use a camera to document her thinking process throughout and then revisit the photos to elaborate on the shifts in her thinking in each phase of her exploration. Through this process Deb learned to move from her tendency toward thematic projects to investigations related solely to the experience of her materials, the white papers. She explored what was a new and challenging process for her, re-representing using drawing and then sculpting with paper. She used the sculptural product of her encounter as a provocation with the 3- to 4-year-old children in her classroom.

Using what you gain from professional development experiences in your work with children can be powerful. It was daring for Deb to introduce materials in new ways with the questions she formed for children that emerged from the insights and questions she generated for herself when working with the same materials. She also questioned whether she could transfer the open attitude she gained in her own exploration to her facilitation of processes with children. She had learned to slow down during her play and wondered if she could hold back on expectations that used to surface for her in relation to curricular planning and facilitating on the spot with children. She gave herself the freedom to remain uncertain (Chaille 2008) about the direction of the process and to facilitate the children's natural flow as they interacted with the white paper provocation.

Deb's documentation captured the nature of her experiences with children, with teacher commentary in the form of interpretations and questions. Here is her introduction of the provocation to children.

Introducing the Provocation. There was a group meeting about this provocation before the display was made available to the children. The teacher discussed her own experiences with white paper to inspire them to freely investigate. Even before the display was set up in the art area, the children were attracted to the materials and how they looked. They were excited to interact with the variety of materials.

Throughout her documentation panel, illustrations of thinking and learning were incorporated with photos, descriptive text, and dialogue among the children and with Deb. Deb paid close attention to subtle aspects of thinking during the paper explorations. For example, what might be observed as just "moving paper around" was interpreted by Deb as a child's exploration with symmetry.

The provocation remained the same into a fourth week. No new materials were added in response as there was continual flow of children entering the exploration for the first time. Their teacher was impressed with the length of time each stayed at the table, talking to one another and manipulating the paper.

During the weeks that the provocation was available for children, Deb noticed that some of the boys used the white papers in ways that tied into their active pretend play:

Eventually it was necessary for this group of children to move to enact upon their ideas about fishing rods and swords. They took their paper to the small blocks center where they became fishermen (ghosties) on a spooky ship—representative of the Halloween season.

Deb closed her panel with two lists communicating what she learned from children about the many ways paper can be explored and ideas for extending those explorations through different threads of inquiry, including language and literacy, the manipulation of paper, and the sounds of paper.

April's Imaginary play with paper

Deb = blue / April = red

What's on top of the placemat? Your breakfast! (She places all of the papers she's collected on top of the placemat). Here's a fork and a spoon. (April hands me two pieces of rolled up paper). What are we eating? Bread. Do we need a fork to eat bread? (I pretend to pick up bread with a fork. So did she). Yes! We do? Did you make this bread? It's delicious! I eat bread all the time. What kind of bread do you like to eat? (She gets up to get more paper). More paper? More bread! We could have soup with our bread. (She pretended to get paper out of the sleeves of plastic and places imaginary bread at our placemats). Bread for you! Bread for me! (She goes back over to the paper and does it again. She picked a piece of paper that looked like a fan (accordion fold)). That looks like good bread. Looks like French toast sticks. Do you want more bread? Yes! Thank you. I'll put it on my plate. That's your placemat. Oh, my placemat? I'll get one for you. Yum, yum! It smells good!

Figure 9.3. A section of a documentation panel from the white paper exploration.

Through this exploration Deb was able to slow down the process to observe more and talk less. She was able to enter into being comfortable with the Big Idea simply being *the manipulation of paper*, without any expectations for a final product.

> The children are interested in finding out what paper can do and they find that paper can make you taller (holding paper overhead) or your arms longer (extending paper from hand), transform, be made into tools, be made into shapes, be inventions, be a book, make noises, make music, be food (breakfast food scenario), be used as hair accessories (bow), feel different (differences in types of paper), make sounds, become an art creation (Haley's symmetry), change sizes (twist, roll, fold, etc.), and help you use your imagination.

Using Small-Format Panels in Deb's School

In Deb's preschool setting, the teachers create documentation panels in PowerPoint or Word documents so that the entire panel is a series of slides or pages. The format makes it easy to create a PDF that can be sent to families digitally by secure email or posted on secure school websites for easy downloading by families, teachers, and administrators.

In the classroom, Deb and her colleagues are creative in the way they post these small-format panels. They insert each page into a plastic 8½" × 11" sleeve and attach these to the walls in the centers where they want to hang the documentation. These are organized in linear fashion on the wall, sometimes with more than one row of PowerPoint pages in order to represent the entire documentation panel. Some classrooms leave these sleeves on their wall in set areas in each learning center so they can replace panels easily as they create new representations of learning. Once a panel is removed, the pages are then inserted into three-ring binders that hold the documentation for an entire project. These binders serve as historical artifacts that are often revisited by children and teachers to reference earlier processes and discover relationships between new and past inquiry. The binders are shared with families or even with children in future years.

From Children's Interests to Children's Thinking

For Further Reflection and Inquiry

By using the COI system, you will learn that documentation is more than hanging children's work on the wall in your classroom. It is a deeply reflective process that promotes a better understanding of your teaching and deepens your knowledge of children's development in your classroom. Revisiting the documentation from your COI observation and planning process will lead to complex thinking as you synthesize and decide the significant features necessary to tell the story of the learning among children and teachers. Your documentation panels are significant tools for developing relationships with families and community members who have connections with your classroom and school. Documentation panels inform families of the life and learning in the classroom, potentially inspiring their engagement in the inquiry and ways they can support their children's development. Documentation panels also represent best practices to early childhood colleagues.

For deeper reflection on how you can use documentation panels with your classroom, try these suggestions:

1. Reflect on the sorts of documentation you have previously shared in your classroom.

2. Think about whether you included teacher commentary.

3. If not, is there commentary you could add to better tell the story of the photos, drawings, or children's products on display in your classroom?

4. Discuss how this changes the representations of learning you are sharing.

5. With your coteachers, teaching team, or director, discuss the distinction between displaying children's work and representing children's learning through documentation panels.

6. When you have gathered observation and planning documentation that represents at least one or more cycles in your inquiry process, create a documentation panel in collaboration with a colleague.

7. Invite families to visit your classroom to give feedback on your documentation panels.

8. Engage in discussions with families about the learning represented in the documentation panels.

CONCLUSION
Continuing the Cycle

Congratulations! You have taken great strides in your journey with emergent inquiry, learning to work with a COI process and documenting your observation and planning thinking on COI forms. Keep this book available to reference as you continue to develop emergent inquiry curriculum. You can refresh your understanding of the many practices and strategies identified for setting up your emergent inquiry classroom environment and organizing small core groups (Chapter 1), for using focused classroom meetings to extend and support long-term emergent inquiry curriculum (Chapter 2), and for planning from observations through a series of intentional planning practices (Chapters 4–7).

Your journey is just beginning. The reflection process captured by the COI Reflective Evaluation form (Chapter 8) guides you to the start of a new cycle generated from your observations of the provocation plan you designed and implemented with children. Each cycle will generate new interpretations and questions as the basis for next steps in a long-term emergent inquiry process. This is a cohesive process, linking the thinking from one cycle to the next. Each new cycle supports children to think and explore with more depth and complexity.

In addition, each cycle will reveal questions and thinking that can diverge into threads of inquiry. You can design inquiry provocations for different small core groups of children around these threads. As you develop threads of inquiry, check that they weave together cohesively with the overarching Big Idea that is guiding your emergent inquiry focus.

Remember that in an emergent inquiry curriculum you will be referring to your state and program early learning standards as a checklist during the times when you reflect back on the processes you've designed and implemented. When you design your curriculum around children's thinking, as described in this book, you will discover that your emergent inquiry curriculum addresses multiple standards, because the long-term project focus integrates content across the learning standard domains. Children will develop deeper understanding through their experiences with the many threads of inquiry that generate from and weave together their thinking over the course of a long-term emergent inquiry process.

Your long-term emergent inquiry project will lead to the development of more than one documentation panel (Chapter 9), each representing the learning over a period of two to four weeks. Synthesizing the ongoing learning is a rewarding and energizing process. Your COI practice will continue to ignite the sense of joy you feel as a teacher and co-learner with children.

Appendices

The COI checklists and COI forms discussed in this book are provided here for documenting your observations, planning, and reflective evaluation.

Appendix 1

COI Observation Record Checklist and COI Observation Record Form

COI Observation Record Checklist

Briefly review your COI Observation Record form for the purpose of developing skill in each of these areas for building an emergent inquiry curriculum.

Amount and nature of the data (photo and written or video)

- ☐ Did you capture sufficient detail to interpret the episode?
- ☐ Did you document connected events to describe a meaningful play episode?
- ☐ Did you follow the connected events even if they moved from place to place?
- ☐ Did you include photographs or video clips
  - › From the level of the child?
  - › Of the steps in the child's thinking process?
  - › Of the child's strategies/techniques with materials?
  - › Of the emotion of the child (if this is significant to the documentation focus)?

Accuracy and ease of use of the data

- ☐ Did you distinguish dialogue from action?
- ☐ Did you distinguish teachers and children?
- ☐ Did you invent methods for recording complex behavior or products?
- ☐ Did you produce a clear descriptive transcript of important processes and products you observed?

Focus on children's thinking and on your thinking (analytic memos)

- ☐ Did you separate your speculations and thinking from your observations?
- ☐ Did you relate children's actions to their possible goals or theories?
- ☐ Did you think about links to previous play episodes in your memos?
- ☐ Did you think about your questions as ideas for plans to extend children's thinking?

Cycle of Inquiry
Observation Record

OR

Tag:

Interpreters:

Date:

AREA:

PARTICIPANTS:

SETUP:

By working with documentation of children's **actions** and **words** we focus our discussions on evidence and de-privatize our discussions about children's thinking. (Reggio Study Group)

NAMES: Distinguish teachers' names from children's.	DESCRIPTION: **WORDS**—Not in parentheses **ACTIONS**—(In parentheses)	MEMOS: Raise your questions about the meanings of children's actions and words. Why did they do/say this? What do they know?

Observation (continued)

By working with documentation of children's actions and words we focus our discussions on evidence and de-privatize our discussions about children's thinking. (Reggio Study Group)

When using video note the start/end time frames of clip you reference in name column.

NAMES: Distinguish teachers' names from children's.	DESCRIPTION: **WORDS**—Not in parentheses **ACTIONS**—(In parentheses)	MEMOS: Raise your questions about the meanings of children's actions and words. Why did they do/say this? What do they know?

Observation (continued)

By working with documentation of children's actions and words we focus our discussing
on evidence and de-privatize our discussions about children's thinking. (Reggio Study Group)
When using video note the start/end time frames of clip you reference in name column.

NAMES: Distinguish teachers' names from children's.	PHOTO IMAGE Insert images that capture the processes of children's play noted in preceding pages. Consider the way the child sees the processes, steps in the child's thinking process, and the child's technique with materials.	MEMOS: Raise your questions about the meanings of children's actions and words. Why did they do/say this? What do they know?

Appendix 2

COI Interpreting Thinking Checklist and COI Interpreting Thinking Form

COI Interpreting Thinking Checklist

Briefly review your COI Interpreting Thinking form for the purpose of developing skill in each of these areas for building an emergent inquiry curriculum.

Focus on children's knowledge and thinking

☐ Did you describe significant (possibly meaningful) events in the children's play?

☐ Did you capture your thoughts about why these events were significant?

☐ Did you interpret events as indicators of the thinking of children, not just their interests or needs?

☐ Did you speculate on the goals behind the actions of the children?

☐ Did you speculate on what knowledge and theories of the world made these actions strategic or sensible to children?

Focus on differing children's perspectives

☐ Did you look at the events from the children's perspectives, to wonder how they experienced things?

☐ Did you describe and question unexpected events that indicate when children see things differently?

Focus on learning opportunities in the play

☐ Did you look ahead to how your ideas might be used in planning?

☐ Did you articulate various hypotheses about opportunities in the play to extend the children's development, knowledge, or understanding?

☐ Did you describe in the narrative what you saw or heard that led you to your ideas?

☐ Did you look back and ahead to see whether you and the children are pursuing distinct threads of inquiry?

Tag:

Interpreters:

Date:

Speculate on what the children are doing and thinking.

In the next two boxes, keep in mind that you're looking for emerging threads of play that have the most potential for advancing play toward children's inquiry. *You are forming a context for interpreting what you saw.*

Write a narrative using as much ***descriptive language*** as possible to tell the reader what you think this play was about. Write freely. Within your description, ***speculate with statements*** like "I think they are doing *X* because of *Y*."

Look at the above paragraph. Imagine you are the child/children you wrote about. Be those children and write what you are thinking. (We ask you to complete this task to help you dig a bit more deeply into the perspective of the child.)

Appendix 3

COI Curriculum Action Plan Checklist and COI Curriculum Action Plan Form

Briefly review your COI Curriculum Action Plan form for the purpose of developing
skill in each of these areas for building an emergent inquiry curriculum.

Checklist for Column I

Exploring hypotheses and questions

☐ Do your action questions pursue or speculate on your better understanding of what children might want to know, gaps in children's knowledge, a child's theory, observed problems, or limits to children's thinking?

☐ Will your questions lead children to pursue their own questions and theories?

☐ Do your action questions about recent play connect with earlier play?

☐ Do your action questions facilitate children to revisit and re-represent their previous experiences and learning?

☐ Will your action questions engage children in collaboration with peers and adults as a community of learners?

☐ Did you discover a thread of inquiry among a small group that can be explored with the whole group?

☐ Do your action questions link together into multifaceted explorations of one Big Idea?

Checklist for Column II

Developing provocation strategies

☐ Do your provocation ideas focus on the questions you posed for each action question?

☐ Did you introduce or shift the materials so that they afford increasing exploration for children to make their thinking visible through expressions with the materials, better understand their ideas, gain new perspectives, or learn properties of the materials?

☐ Did you plan statements that might provoke conversations among the children to further explore their thinking during the new play?

☐ Did you plan guiding questions to facilitate conversations among the children to further explore their thinking and/or pose their own question during the new play?

Cycle of Inquiry
Curriculum Action Plan

Tag:

Interpreters:

Date:

EXPLORE WHAT YOU WANT TO PURSUE WITH THE CHILDREN

This is divergent thinking. Be creative but stay grounded in your observations and speculations about the children's play. Looking back at your interpretations of their play, explore different ways to challenge, guide, or question the children to extend their play into the areas you think they are working with. These can become the emerging threads of the curriculum you are developing with the children.

Column I—Action questions: You develop your curriculum from questions you want to pursue about children's thinking or things you think the children want to understand. **Below, write 3 or more questions you could act on to develop threads in your curriculum. You are not creating a sequence of sessions. Each question represents one next possible session with children.**	**Column II—Provocation strategies:** You guide the curriculum by provoking thought—by providing opportunities and experiences, that deeply engage the children, draw forth their competencies and build mastery. **For each action question in Column I, record the materials and productive questions or statements you will use to guide a next play session centered on your action question. List the many diverse materials, along with several productive questions/statements, that will help children experiment with and extend their theories.**
1	
2	
3	

Check for Big Ideas. Before you begin planning, reflect on the questions you are pursuing with the children. Pull in the standards. From your perspective as a "knowledgeable other," do you see a bigger picture forming? Jot it down here.

Appendix 4

COI Inquiry Provocation Plan Checklist
and COI Inquiry Provocation Plan Form

COI Inquiry Provocation Plan Checklist

Briefly review your COI Inquiry Provocation Plan form for the purpose of developing skill in each of these areas for building an emergent inquiry curriculum.

Framing implementation by aligning an action question with evidence of children's thinking

☐ Did you design an action question by revisiting and reframing your action questions in your Curriculum Action Plan form?

☐ Did you pinpoint evidence in your COI Observation Record form directly related to your question?

☐ Did you develop a rationale linking your thinking and reasoning about your action question to the children's thinking?

☐ Did you include a Big Idea that links this provocation to previous and possible future provocations? (The Big Idea you note here might clarify or reframe the Big Idea/s from your previous planning forms.)

Inquiry provocation plan: Materials, environment setup, and productive questions and statements

☐ Did you choose materials that afford increasing exploration for children to make their thinking visible through expressions with the materials, work toward a better understanding of their ideas, gain new perspectives, or learn properties of the materials?

☐ Did you design a way to set up the materials that will invite children to play and guide them in their play so that teachers do less and children do more?

☐ Will children be able to read your presentation of materials in a way that shows them how to enter and respond in relation to your action question?

☐ Did you design questions and provocation statements that will lead children to pursue their own questions and theories?

Procedures

☐ Did you organize a fully-developed procedure in which you considered
  › How you will get children ready for the experience?
  › How you will introduce the provocation processes, which might include materials, questions, conversations, modeling, listing, or diagramming?
  › How you plan for the session with children to close?

☐ Did you describe how you will document the children's play?

Cycle of Inquiry
Inquiry Provocation Plan

Tag:
Planners:

Date:

BRING YOUR IDEAS INTO A PLAN

This is convergent thinking. Use the ideas you've generated from thinking about the children's play to create a planned intervention. Use enough details in each box so that another person could set up and guide the play session that you are planning.

AREA:
PARTICIPANTS:
DATE & TIME:

ACTION QUESTIONS: Keep your intentions clear.

Revisit your action questions. Which question or questions are you pursuing?
Do you see already see a clear thread emerging in the play?

GROUND THE PLAN IN YOUR OBSERVATIONS AND SPECULATIONS ABOUT THE CHILDREN'S THINKING.

RATIONALE: Look back at your observations, memos, and interpretations. Write an interpretation that states why you chose to pursue this action question with children.

EVIDENCE: Revisit the COI Observation Record form and copy selections that pinpoint the actions and words that helped you formulate your questions.

BIG IDEA

Check for Big Ideas. Before you begin planning, reflect on the questions you are pursuing with the children. Do you see a bigger picture forming? Try to see the ways that any of the threads you identify remain consistent from cycle to cycle. If you see a way they link together in any way—you likely have identified a Big Idea/s. Note your thoughts here.

BRING YOUR IDEAS INTO A PLAN

This is convergent thinking. Use the ideas you've generated from thinking about the children's play to create a planned intervention. Use enough details in each box so that another person could set up and guide the play session that you are planning.

DESIGN THE PROVOCATION. Align this with the questions you are pursuing with the children.

MATERIALS: Choose the materials for their affordances and their ability to provoke theory building in the children.	SETUP: Design the play environment to be the third teacher and to invite the children to explore. Write a description of how you will set up the environment so that the materials will guide this play session, so the children will know what to do as they read the set up. The goal is for the children to do more and for teachers to do less.	QUESTIONS: Think ahead about *the many* productive questions you might use when you interact with the children during their play.

OUTLINE YOUR PROCEDURES. Number the steps 1, 2, 3, etc.

How will you introduce the children to your provocation? Will you start with a focused small core group discussion or a focused classroom meeting with the whole class, invite children to explore the materials in a center, invite children to represent their thinking with the materials, enter into a dialogue with the children? These are some of the many strategies you might use. Think through what you will do, including **how you will document the play** so you can evaluate what happened and plan from it. Write your procedures so that another teacher could reasonably follow them.

Appendix 5

COI Reflective Evaluation Checklist and COI Reflective Evaluation Form

COI Reflective Evaluation Checklist

Briefly review your COI Reflective Evaluation form for the purpose of developing
skill in each of these areas for building an emergent inquiry curriculum

Evaluate learning

☐ Does your description of the children's reaction provide enough detail for the reader to visualize children's strategies and thinking in the context of a particular learning environment?

☐ Did you describe what the activity was like for the children with enough detail that the reader (you, your coteacher, an administrator) can clearly visualize and understand the events from your perspective?

☐ When you state that learning has occurred, do your examples provide evidence from specific observed interactions that led to the knowledge construction? (Sometimes you might observe thinking that doesn't develop new knowledge, so don't record that.)

☐ Does the learning you note relate to your action question from the COI Inquiry Provocation Plan form?

☐ Did you list relevant learning standards from *all* domains of learning for your state and age group?

☐ Did you write a statement for each standard you noted that shows the way it connects to the learning outcomes from this play session?

Evaluate implementation and documentation

☐ Did you describe ways the session matched or didn't match your expectations with enough detail that the reader (you, your coteacher, an administrator) can clearly visualize and understand the events from your perspective?

☐ Did you describe the ways the materials and setup influenced the children's thinking and learning?

☐ Did you describe the ways your facilitation strategies were successful or need improvement?

Projecting next steps forward in the curriculum

☐ Did you reflect on the children's current goals and ideas and describe the best possible next learning steps in detail?

Cycle of Inquiry
Reflective Evaluation

REVISIT THE SESSION AND EVALUATE IT AS A LEARNING EXPERIENCE
Emergent curricula give children learning experiences and opportunities to develop their
competencies, their theories, and their sense of mastery over knowledge, circumstances, and skills.
Reflect on this session and evaluate its worth for both the children and the teachers.

AREA:
PARTICIPANTS:
DATE & TIME:

CHILDREN'S REACTION: Do you have evidence that the children were engaged? Think about and
describe what the experience was like for the children in ways that describe their goals and their strategies
for meeting those goals. Were children cooperative? Did they experience collaboration?

LEARNING: Do you have evidence that the children learned?

HOW DID THE SESSION MATCH YOUR INTENTIONS? Think about and describe in detail what the experience was like
for you and how the experience aligned with the rationale you presented in your COI Inquiry Provocation Plan form.

Tag: **Date:**

WHAT DID YOU LEARN ABOUT FACILITATING PLAY? Think about the influence of the materials and setup on the children and about the influence of your questions or provocation statements.

WHAT NEXT? How will you build on this learning? In what ways can you provide differentiated support for diverse learners?

STANDARDS CHECKLIST: What curricular standards were met during this session?

DOCUMENTATION. How effective was your choice of documentation for this session? Note your thoughts on other methods to use that would be more helpful for your needs. Develop a plan, as needed, to improve your own skill with documentation.

References

Baker, M., & G.S. Davila. 2018. "Inquiry Is Play: Playful Participatory Research (Voices)." *Young Children* 73 (5). www.naeyc.org/resources/pubs /yc/nov2018/inquiry-is-play-playful-participatory -research.

Bodrova, E., & D.J. Leong. 2007. *Tools of the Mind: The Vygotskyan Approach to Early Childhood Education*. 2nd. ed. Upper Saddle River, NJ: Pearson Education/Merrill.

Boehm, A.E., & R.A. Weinberg. 1996. *The Classroom Observer: Developing Observation Skills in Early Childhood Settings*. 3rd ed. New York: Teachers College Press.

Broderick, J.T., & S.B. Hong. 2005. "Inquiry in Early Childhood Teacher Education: Reflections on Practice." *The Constructivist* 16 (1): 1–30.

Broderick, J.T., & S.B. Hong. 2011. "Introducing the Cycle of Inquiry System: A Reflective Inquiry Practice for Early Childhood Teacher Development." *Early Childhood Research and Practice* 13 (2). https://ecrp.uiuc.edu/v13n2 /broderick.html.

Bronfenbrenner, U., & S.J. Ceci. 1994. "Nature- Nurture Reconceptualized in Developmental Perspective: A Bioecological Model." *Psychological Review* 101 (4): 568–86.

Brooks, J.G. 2011. *Big Science for Growing Minds: Constructivist Classrooms for Young Thinkers*. New York: Teachers College Press.

Carter, M.. 2018. "The Thinking Lens: Making Thinking Visible." In *From Teaching to Thinking: A Pedagogy for Reimagining Our Work*, A. Pelo & M. Carter, 258–79. Lincoln, NE: Exchange Press.

Chant, R., R. Moes, & M. Ross. 2009. "Curriculum Instruction and Teacher Empowerment: Supporting Invitational Education with a Creative Problem Solving Model." *Journal of Invitational Theory and Practice* 15: 55–67.

Chaille, C. 2008. *Constructivism Across the Curriculum: Big Ideas as Inspiration*. Boston: Allyn and Bacon.

Castle, K. 2012. *Early Childhood Teacher Research: From Questions to Results*. New York: Routledge.

Copple, C., & S. Bredekamp. 2009. *Developmentally Appropriate Practice in Early Childhood Programs: Serving Children from Birth through Age 8*. 3rd ed. Washington, DC: NAEYC.

Crain, W. 2011. *Theories of Development: Concepts and Applications*. 6th ed. New York: Psychology Press.

Curtis, D. 2017. *Really Seeing Children*. Lincoln, NE: Exchange Press.

DeVries, R., B. Zan, C. Hildebrandt, R. Edmiaston, & C. Sales. 2002. *Developing Constructivist Early Childhood Curriculum: Practical Principles and Activities*. New York: Teachers College Press.

Duckworth, E. 2006. *"The Having of Wonderful Ideas" and Other Essays on Teaching and Learning*. New York: Teachers College Press.

Edwards, C., L. Gandini, & G. Forman, eds. 1998. *The Hundred Languages of Children: The Reggio Emilia Approach to Early Childhood Education*. 2nd. ed. Greenwich, CT: Ablex.

Edwards, C., L. Gandini, & G. Forman, eds. 2012. *The Hundred Languages of Children: The Reggio Emilia Approach to Early Childhood Education*. 3rd. ed. Santa Barbara, CA: Praeger.

Engel, S. 2011. "Children's Need to Know: Curiosity in Schools." *Harvard Educational Review* 81 (4): 625–784.

Evans, L.M. 2019. "The Power of Science: Using Inquiry Thinking to Enhance Learning in a Dual Language Preschool Classroom." *Young Children* 74 (2): 14–23.

Fisher, K.R. 2011. "Exploring the Mechanism of Guided Play in Preschoolers' Developing Geometric Shape Concepts." Doctoral diss., Temple University (UMI 3440076).

Forman, G., & Hall, H. 2005. "Wondering with Children: The Importance of Observation in Early Education." *Early Childhood Research and Practice* 7 (2). https://ecrp.illinois.edu/v7n2/forman.html.

Forman, G., J. Langley, M. Oh, & L.Wrisley. 1998. "The City in the Snow: Applying the Multisymbolic Approach in Massachusetts." In *The Hundred Language of Children: The Reggio Emilia Approach—Advanced Reflection*, 2nd ed., eds. C. Edwards, L. Gandini, & G. Forman, 359–74. Greenwich, CT: Ablex.

Fosnot, C. 2005. *Constructivism: Theory, Perspectives and Practice*. New York: Teachers College Press.

Fuchs, L.S., & S.L. Deno. 1991. "Paradigmatic Distinctions Between Instructionally Relevant Measurement Models." *Exceptional Children* 57 (6): 488–500.

Gandini, L., & J. Goldhaber. 2001. "Two Reflections About Documentation." In *Bambini: The Italian Approach to Infant/Toddler Care*, eds. L. Gandini & C.P. Edwards, 124–45. New York: Teachers College Press.

Ginsberg, H., & S. Opper. 1988. *Piaget's Theory of Intellectual Development*. 3rd ed. Upper Saddle River, NJ: Pearson.

Giudici, C, C. Rinaldi, & M. Krechevsky. 2001. *Making Learning Visible: Children as Individual and Group Learners*. Boston, MA: Project Zero, Harvard Graduate School of Education.

Hamre, B., B. Hatfield, R. Pianta, & F. Jamil. 2014. "Evidence for General and Domain-Specific Elements of Teacher–Child Interactions: Associations with Preschool Children's Development." *Child Development* 85 (3): 1257–74. doi:10.1111/cdev.12184.

Hill, L., A. Stremmel, & V. Fu. 2005. *Teaching as Inquiry: Rethinking Curriculum in Early Childhood Education*. Boston: Pearson.

Hong, S. 1998. "Documentation-Panel-Making and Revisiting Using Technology to Enhance Observation and Instruction Skills in Student Teachers." Doctoral diss., University of Massachusetts Amherst (UMI No. 9841879).

Hong, S., & G. Forman. 2000. "What Constitutes a Good Documentation Panel and How to Achieve It?" *Canadian Children* 25 (2): 26–31.

Jones, E. 2012. "The Emergence of Emergent Curriculum." *Young Children* 67 (2): 62–66.

Jones, E., K. Evans, & K.S. Rencken. 2001. *The Lively Kindergarten: Emergent Curriculum in Action*. Washington, DC: NAEYC.

Lange, A., K. Brenneman, & H. Mano. 2019. *Teaching STEM in the Preschool Classroom*. New York: Teachers College Press.

Martens, M.L. 1999. "Productive Questions: Tools for Supporting Constructive Learning." *Science and Children* 36 (8): 26–53.

McDonald, P. 2019. "Observing, Planning, Guiding: How an Intentional Teacher Meets Standards Through Play." In *Serious Fun: How Guided Play Extends Children's Learning*, eds. M. Masterson & H. Bohart, 20–33. Washington, DC: NAEYC.

McLean, K., M. Jones, & C. Schaper. 2015. "Children's Literature as an Invitation to Science Inquiry in Early Childhood Education." *Australasian Journal of Early Childhood* 40 (4): 49–56. https://journals.sagepub.com/doi/pdf/10.1177/183693911504000407.

NAEYC. 2009. "Developmentally Appropriate Practice in Early Childhood Programs Serving Children from Birth through Age 8." Position statement. Washington, DC: NAEYC. www.naeyc.org/sites/default/files/globally-shared/downloads/PDFs/resources/position-statements/PSDAP.pdf.

National Research Council. 1999. *How People Learn: Brain, Mind, Experience, and School.* Washington, DC: National Academies Press.

National Research Council. 2012. *A Framework for K–12 Science Education: Practices, Crosscutting Concepts, and Core Ideas.* Washington, DC: National Academies Press.

Nilsen, B.A. 2016. *Week by Week: Plans for Documenting Children's Development.* 7th ed. Independence, KY: Cengage.

Piaget, J. (1926) 1997. *A Child's Conception of the World.* New York: Routledge.

Piaget, J. (1947) 2003. *The Psychology of Intelligence.* New York: Routledge.

Pianta, R.C., & B.K. Hamre. 2009. "Conceptualization, Measurement, and Improvement of Classroom Processes: Standardized Observation Can Leverage Capacity." *Educational Researcher* 38 (2): 109–19.

Rosenthal, J.L. 2018. "Teacher Candidates in the Garden." *Science Activities* 55 (1–2): 20–27. https://doi.org/10.1080/00368121.2017.1403875.

Schaeffer, R. 2016. "Teacher Inquiry on the Influence of Materials on Children's Learning." Voices of Practitioners. *Young Children* 71 (5): 64–73. www.naeyc.org/resources/pubs/yc/nov2016/teacher-inquiry-materials.

Silveira, B., & D. Curtis. 2018. "Look, Listen, Learn. Where Does the Rain Go? Considering the Teacher's Role in Children's Discoveries." *Teaching Young Children* 11 (5): 22–23. www.naeyc.org/resources/pubs/tyc/aug2018/considering-teachers-role-childrens-discoveries.

Smith, D., & J. Goldhaber. 2004. *Poking, Pinching and Pretending: Documenting Toddlers' Exploration with Clay.* St. Paul, MN: Redleaf Press.

Stacey, S. 2009. *Emergent Curriculum in Early Childhood Settings: From Theory to Practice.* St. Paul, MN: Redleaf Press.

Stacey, S. 2011. *The Unscripted Classroom: Emergent Curriculum in Action.* St. Paul, MN: Redleaf Press.

Stremmel, A. 2007. "The Value of Teacher Research: Nurturing Professional and Personal Growth through Inquiry." *Voices of Practitioners* 2 (3): 1–9.

Topal, C. 1998. *Children, Clay and Sculpture.* Worcester, MA: Davis Publications.

Treffinger, D.J., & S.G. Isaksen. 2005. "Creative Problem Solving: The History, Development, Implications for Gifted Education and Talent Development." *Gifted Child Quarterly* 49 (4): 342–53.

Vecchi, V. 2010. *Art and Creativity in Reggio Emilia: Exploring the Role and Potential of Ateliers in Early Childhood Education.* New York: Routledge.

Vygotsky, L. (1934) 1986. *Thought and Language.* Boston: MIT Press.

Weatherly, L., V. Oleson, & L.R. Kistner. 2017. "Over the Fence: Engaging Preschoolers and Families in a Yearlong STEAM Investigation." *Young Children* 72 (5): 44–50. www.naeyc.org/resources/pubs/yc/nov2017/over-the-fence.

Wien, C.A., ed. 2008. *Emergent Curriculum in the Primary Classroom: Interpreting the Reggio Emilia Approach in Schools.* New York: Teachers College Press.

Wien, C.A., V. Guyevskey., & N. Berdoussis. 2011. "Learning to Document in Reggio-Inspired Education." *Early Childhood Research & Practice* 13 (2). https://ecrp.illinois.edu/v13n2/wien.html.

Wien, C.A., & D. Halls. 2018. "'Is There a Chick in There?' Kindergartners' Changing Thoughts on Life in an Egg." *Young Children* 73 (1): 6–14. www.naeyc.org/resources/pubs/yc/mar2018/kindergartners-changing-thoughts-life-egg.

Wood, D., J.S. Bruner, & G. Ross. 1976. "The Role of Tutoring in Problem Solving." *Journal of Child Psychology and Psychiatry* 17 (2): 89–100.

Resources for Further Study

Elstgeest, J. 2001. "The Right Question at the Right Time." In *Primary Science: Taking the Plunge*, 2nd ed., ed. H. Wynne, 25–27. Portsmouth, NH: Heinemann.

Flower, L, D.L. Wallace, L. Norris, & R.E. Burnett. 1994. *Making Thinking Visible: Writing, Collaborative Planning, and Classroom Inquiry*. Urbana, IL: National Council of Teachers of English.

Forman, G., & B. Fyfe. 1998. "Negotiated Learning Through Design, Documentation, and Discourse." In *The Hundred Languages of Children: The Reggio Emilia Approach—Advanced Reflections*, 2nd ed., eds. C. Edwards, L. Gandini, & G. Forman, 239–60. Greenwich, CT: Ablex.

Forman, G., & L. Gandini, prods. 2006. *An Amusement Park for Birds*. DVD. Amherst, MA: Performanetics Press.

Helm, J.H., & L. Katz. 2011. *Young Investigators: The Project Approach in the Early Years*. 2nd ed. New York: Teachers College Press.

Hendricks, J. 1997. *First Steps Toward Teaching the Reggio Way*. Upper Saddle River, NJ: Prentice Hall.

Jones, E., & J. Nimmo. 1998. *Emergent Curriculum*. Washington, DC: NAEYC.

Katz, L.G., & S.C. Chard. 2000. *Engaging Children's Minds: The Project Approach*. 2nd ed. Stamford, CT: Ablex.

Acknowledgments

We very much appreciate our families for believing in our work and hanging in there as we wrote and edited. We value our editors at NAEYC for their constructive insights and conviction that our work is meaningful for the field of early childhood. Their expertise made the editing a smooth process.

We are grateful for the opportunity to have so many people supporting our journey over the years in the development of the cycle of inquiry system and its use in early childhood settings. So many teachers, preservice teachers, children, families, and colleagues have played a role in this work.

From our years at the University of Massachusetts Amherst, we would both like to thank our mentor, George Forman, for guiding our thinking about the thinking of children. In addition, our work in the Early Childhood Laboratory School with Dotty Meyer guided our understanding of emergent curriculum in the classroom. Big thanks to Cissy Walker for early reading and recommendations.

At East Tennessee State University, we appreciate the ability to share the work of teachers, preservice teachers, and children from the Child Study Center. We are grateful for former director Beverly Wiginton for inviting us into the classrooms and for the permission families provided for sharing their children's inquiry. In particular, we thank Joy Matson, Yolanda Steadman, and Lynn Lodien for their collaboration on the bluegrass study. Special thanks are extended to Leona Mathes and Lara Beth Fair, two preservice teachers and musicians who committed to facilitating our understanding of bluegrass and old-time music. In addition, Megan Felker is to be complimented for her help with the creative facilitation of materials and Lonny Finley for his expertise as a musician in this study.

Su Lorencen, Gloria Reilly, and Jackie Vaughn helped with many of the photos for sections of this book. Students in the creative development classes, including teachers and directors from Rainbow Riders in Blacksburg, Virginia, and the director of Highland Plaza United Methodist Preschool in Hixon, Tennessee, guided us with insights on the use of the COI.

We learned so much when working with the former laboratory preschool director and teachers at Appalachian State University and appreciate being able to share insights from them: Ariel Ford, Meg Hampton, Jessica Carter, Jenn Marsh Klutz, and Christelle Marsh. We also appreciate the creative insights of Mike Garrett, who studied and believed in our work during his time as an early childhood doctoral fellow at East Tennessee State University.

At the University of Michigan–Dearborn we thank the Early Childhood Education Center teachers who were willing to use and reflect on the COI system to develop their curriculum with children for over 10 years. Their guidance of preservice teachers in the classroom supported our work over the years and provided examples we have shared here. In particular, we thank Christina Raffoul and Freda Shatara, preservice teachers who are brave in their sharing of the incinerator project they implemented in the classroom of teachers Danielle Muehlenbein and Brooke Holman. Also, we greatly appreciate the Early Childhood Education Center families who provided permission for their children to be included in this book.

About the Authors

Jane Tingle Broderick, EdD, is a professor of Early Childhood Education at East Tennessee State University, where she co-coordinates the Early Childhood PhD Program and the Early Childhood Education Emergent Inquiry Certificate Program. She has taught in early childhood for more than 20 years.

Jane is also a visual artist with a BFA from Pratt Institute. She served as an atelierista and documentarian at the Reggio-inspired Early Childhood Laboratory School at UMass, Amherst during her doctoral studies. She and her colleague Seong Bock Hong developed the COI system for use in their teaching and research projects and have presented their COI work at NAEYC and other conferences.

Jane is a long-time member of the Association of Constructivist Teaching, serving as a board member for three years. She lives in Johnson City, Tennessee, with her husband, who is a woodworker. They have two children who are both committed to working with the earth through sustainable landscaping and farming.

Seong Bock Hong, EdD, is a professor of Early Childhood Education at the University of Michigan–Dearborn, where she teaches graduate and undergraduate early childhood courses. She was the faculty director of the Early Childhood Education Center, a university lab school, from 2012 to 2017. She served as an interim director and documentarian at the Reggio-inspired Early Childhood Laboratory School during her doctoral studies at UMass, Amherst.

Seong Bock co-hosted "The Wonder of Learning—Hundred Languages of Children" exhibition in Ann Arbor, Michigan, in 2017. She has received a number of awards for her distinguished professional achievement, including the inaugural Rosalyn Saltz Collegiate Professorship award in 2012 and the University of Michigan Diversity Leadership award in 2010. She currently serves as president of the Association for Constructivist Teaching.

Seong Bock and her husband, a retired chemistry professor, live in Novi, Michigan. They have two children who are working professionals in medicine and engineering.

More Resources to Enhance Your Curriculum

Serious Fun

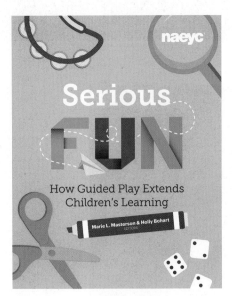

Print: Item 1137 • E-book: Item e1137
2019 • 144 pages

Guided play is a powerful tool educators can use to help preschoolers and kindergartners learn essential knowledge and skills in the context of playful situations. Young children's natural curiosity and dynamic imaginations can lead to exciting and meaningful learning opportunities. Discover how to provide guided play experiences along with opportunities for unstructured play to support children's knowledge in key areas and their lifelong enjoyment and pursuit of learning.

Big Questions for Young Minds

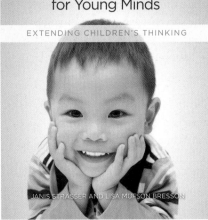

Print: Item 1132 • E-book: Item e1132
2017 • 160 pages

Questions are powerful tools, especially in the classroom. Asking rich, thoughtful questions can spark young children's natural curiosity and illuminate a whole new world of possibility and insight. But what are "big" questions, and how do they encourage children to think deeply? With this intentional approach—rooted in Bloom's Taxonomy—teachers working with children ages 3 through 6 will discover how to meet children at their individual developmental levels and stretch their thinking. With the guidance in this book as a cornerstone in your day-to-day teaching practices, learn how to be more intentional in your teaching, scaffold children's learning, and promote deeper understanding.

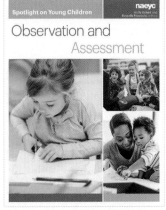

Item 2842 • 2018 • 112 pages

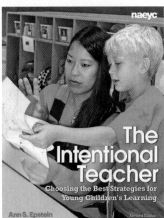

Item 1120 • 2014 • 304 pages

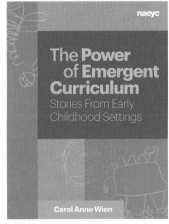

Item 181 • 2014 • 152 pages